SESSIONS WITH EZEKIEL

Smyth & Helwys Publishing, Inc.
6316 Peake Road
Macon, Georgia 31210-3960
1-800-747-3016
© 2022 by Tyler Tankersley

Library of Congress Cataloging-in-Publication Data

Names: Tankersley, Tyler, author.
Title: Sessions with Ezekiel : holiness and hope / by Tyler Tankersley.
Description: Macon, GA : Smyth & Helwys Publishing, 2022. | Includes
bibliographical references.
Identifiers: LCCN 2022018332 | ISBN 9781641733816 (paperback)
Subjects: LCSH: Bible. Ezekiel--Textbooks.
Classification: LCC BS1545.55 .T36 2022 | DDC 224/.406--dc23/eng/20220615
LC record available at https://lccn.loc.gov/2022018332

Sessions *with*
Ezekiel

● ● ● *Holiness* and *Hope*

Tyler Tankersley

SMYTH&HELWYS
PUBLISHING INCORPORATED   MACON, GEORGIA

Also by Tyler Tankersley

Preaching the Word: Galatians

To Henry, Owen, and Charlotte
May you believe that God is with you and that God is for you,
May you believe that an alternative neighborly ethic is ever possible,
May you believe that dry bones can live again,
And may you know that your father is so proud of you
simply for your being you.

And to Jess, my anam cara and partner,
thank you for the unending grace and wisdom.
Also, are you free this Saturday night?

Acknowledgments

I am especially grateful for the biblical scholars who have long labored in the strange and unfamiliar world of Ezekiel. Throughout my work on this project, I was especially guided by the wisdom and insights of Daniel Block, Nancy Bowen, Margaret Odell, and Christopher Wright. I am grateful for the ways they have maintained fidelity to the biblical text and written with winsome grace and creativity.

I am also grateful to the wonderful congregation of Ardmore Baptist Church in Winston-Salem, North Carolina, and especially to those who participated in the Winter 2022 Pastor's Bible Study as we journeyed through Ezekiel together. It is a joy to walk alongside the people of Ardmore Baptist, and the Lord uses them to continually teach me more about goodness and grace.

Thank you to Keith Gammons and Michael McCullar for the invitation to contribute to this series and to Leslie Andres for her fine editorial work. Any lingering mistakes belong to me alone.

Finally, thank you to all who labor in communities of faith teaching Scripture to small groups in classrooms, on sofas in living rooms, in local coffee shops amidst the bustle of life, or via Zoom as you have to ask people to, yet again, please mute their mics. The idea that a small group of believers can gather around a text written thousands of years ago and hear a fresh word from God is a miracle that should never be taken lightly. Thank you for that holy, sacred work.

Contents

Introducing Ezekiel

Jewish rabbis tell an ancient story of a child who rummaged through some objects at his teacher's home and came across a written copy of the book of Ezekiel. As the child began to read the story, he came to the fantastical opening vision of the prophet's calling by the River Chebar. Immediately, fire sprang from the page and consumed the child. The ancient rabbis believed that reading Ezekiel without the proper amount of maturity was not merely confusing but also dangerous, and they often restricted students from studying Ezekiel until they were at least thirty years old (Duguid, 17).

Most people rarely, if ever, spend time in the book of Ezekiel. It is filled with disturbing images, bizarre rhetoric, and foreign references that may render it both confusing and inaccessible to a modern audience. Ezekiel does not lend itself well to cutesy sermon series or easy-to-digest spiritual maxims. It is difficult to pluck any specific passage from Ezekiel out of context and expect to garner an understanding of the book's overall message. Maybe the rabbis were on to something with their warning. Maybe only the wisdom and discernment that comes with age can open our perspective to the message of this enigmatic book. We would do well to hear the "spirit of the law" and proceed with humility and caution.

Who Was Ezekiel?

My own fascination with Ezekiel began in seminary. I grew up in a church context in which we rarely read the Hebrew prophets. The only time I ever remember hearing sermons from the prophetic books of the Old Testament was when they were cast in the role of predictors of Jesus' coming or when a fundamentalist revival preacher was transposing current events onto ancient prophetic oracles.

However, when I went to seminary, I began to study the prophets not as props for preconceived ideas but as writings unto themselves with their own conflicts, characters, narratives, and contexts. Ezekiel captured my imagination unlike any other book. I had some fleeting familiarity with the passage about the dry bones (Ezek 37:1-14), but everything else was completely novel to me. As I began to dig into the story and do the work of understanding Ezekiel in his own setting, a resonance began to rise within me.

I felt the call to ministry at an early age. I watched the pastors and youth ministers of my adolescence (including my own father) and saw how they held positions of high regard in our community and how their jobs equipped them to live into a culture in which the church was one of the centers of our communal life. In many ways, I expected to simply slide into that kind of life and imagined myself serving in a similar role. However, during seminary it became clear that the world of the generations before me was quickly slipping away. We are living in a time of rapid and exponential change for the Christian church. The role of the church in many people's lives is greatly diminished, and thousands of people leave the church altogether every year. My professors in seminary began to practice brutal honesty with us and discussed how we all needed to find alternative ways to support any potential future families we may have because full-time vocational ministry was a rapidly disappearing career option. Most of the people with whom I graduated seminary are no longer working in church contexts but have adapted the nature of their calling to include a myriad of other ways to lead. Surviving this ever-changing landscape requires pastors and spiritual leaders be creative, entrepreneurial, and innovative in their approaches to both speaking truth and caring for hurting congregations.

This is exactly why Ezekiel is such a prescient and relevant book for our world. We are told in the book of Ezekiel that the prophet came from a priestly family. Scholars even believe that Ezekiel's father, Buzi, was a priest in the Jerusalem temple. Ezekiel's name reflects the theological convictions of his parents: "May God (-el) make strong (ezeki-)" (Bowen, 3). Coming from a priestly family, Ezekiel would likely have expected to walk in his father's footsteps and assume the role of clergy for the people of Jerusalem. Perhaps he imagined himself donning the accoutrements and garb that priests wore. He may have envisioned administering liturgical sacrifices in the temple for his neighbors and friends. However, in 597 BCE, all of that changed. That's the year that King Nebuchadrezzar II of

Babylon began a military and cultural assault on the vassal state of Judah. Babylon began by sending the upper crust of Judahite society into exile in Babylon. Ancient empires employed this common tactic in an effort to "brain drain" a conquered people (Darr, 3). Ezekiel found himself in a foreign land, separated from the temple and devoid of the future he had imagined for himself. Like many seminary graduates and congregational leaders in our world, Ezekiel had to creatively imagine how he could minister to his community in an unfamiliar and mysterious context. As Christopher Wright says, "What we may fail to appreciate is the abrupt disorientation and massive reorientation that it must have taken for one brought up as a priest to suddenly find himself called to be a prophet" (Wright 2001, 25).

Who Was Ezekiel's Audience?

Ezekiel's book is written to the exiles in Babylon. From Ezekiel and other biblical prophetic texts, we know that the people of Judah had been separated not just by exile but also by ideology. Ezekiel has nothing positive to say to about the Judeans who had remained in Jerusalem, and he spends some of his book raking them over the coals. Ezekiel even seems to blame the Judeans left in Jerusalem for the exile itself and for God's apparent abandonment of God's people. It is important for us to recognize that Ezekiel's polemic perspective is just one among many. Surely, there are other voices who would view the causes of the exile differently. It does not diminish the holiness of this text for us to acknowledge the human and polemical nature of its worldview (Darr, 7).

The book is addressed to exiles, forced migrants, people who have had everything they ever knew laid waste by the destructive forces of empire. They find themselves in a foreign land among people who speak a foreign language and worship foreign gods. Ezekiel and the exilic community likely experienced both the initial ordeal of the siege of Jerusalem and the exile but also the continuous trauma of being removed from their land and temple. Exile is about a fundamental, bedrock loss of identity. As the Chilean-American author Ariel Dorfman writes, "Those who have never suffered the iniquities of exile cannot possibly understand the significance, the gravitas, of a mattress" (48). The meaning of the book of Ezekiel will be missed by anybody who does not attempt to understand the perspective that accompanies such tremendous and monumental loss. We can see the pain and trauma of the experience of exile in the controversial Psalm 137:

> O daughter Babylon, you devastator!
> Happy shall they be who pay you back
>> what you have done to us!
> Happy shall they be who take your little ones
>> and dash them against the rock! (Ps 137:8-9)

People who are in the majority demographics of a nation or culture will likely find the book of Ezekiel strange, alien, and off-putting. Ezekiel is attempting to grapple with the existential questions that accompany loss and upheaval. Walter Brueggemann says that exile is "the experience of knowing that one is an alien, and perhaps even in a hostile environment where the dominant values run counter to one's own" (1997, 115). Psychologically processing such trauma can lead people to images that are repellent and discomforting. Ezekiel certainly has its fair share of disturbing passages. This prophet compares false idols to balls of feces (6:4), refuses to mourn the death of his own life just to prove a point (24:15-27), and uses sexually violent images (16:1-63). (Ezekiel 16 is not one of the passages that will be explored in-depth in this book, but for a resource that illuminates the biblical texts that contain disturbingly violent imagery against women, see Renita J. Weems, *Battered Love: Marriage, Sex, and Violence in the Hebrew Prophets*.) However, the book of Ezekiel is important because it reminds us of the aspects of God that we may tend to ignore in light of our affluence and ease. Ezekiel teaches that God is sovereign, that God is holy, and that God does not tolerate either idolatry or injustice. Ezekiel forces us to reckon with the strangeness and set-apart nature of God's holiness, reflecting that God will not be contained by our dogmas, platitudes, or preconceived notions.

More scholars are beginning to read Ezekiel as way of processing the trauma of exile. Psychologists identify two distinct experiences of trauma: powerlessness and disruption. The nation of Judah was overpowered by the Babylonian Empire, and the cultural marks of being an Israelite were severely disrupted. When a people experience trauma, they tend to seek out narratives and perspectives that provide them with a sense of meaning amid chaos. The prophet/priest Ezekiel seeks to provide his people with foundations based on theological categories: the redemption of Jerusalem, the resumption of the temple's position, and the honor of a holy God. Ezekiel seeks to help his fellow exiles come to terms with their shattered assumptions and provide them with an alternative mental framework from which to process their collective trauma (Bowen, xvi–xvii).

Ezekiel believes that the blame for the experience of exile lies on the shoulders of the people themselves. This position may seem like victim blaming or self-hatred, and certainly we should always advocate for victims against systems that perpetuate oppression and injustice. But there is something liberating about a people group taking upon themselves the reasons for their current exile. In his book *A Biblical Theology of Exile*, Daniel Smith-Christopher argues that the Judeans' self-blame for the exile in the book of Ezekiel is a way of retaining agency and removing power from the hands of the Babylonians. It further provides hope that a fractured relationship can be healed. He writes, "After all, if one's suffering is because of one's own oversights, and not because of the power of the emperor and his armies, then this holds out considerably more hope about a future restoration" (Smith-Christopher, 81).

The Structure of the Book of Ezekiel

The book of Ezekiel is an intentionally crafted piece of literature that uses various genres to tell a story. It also can be divided into three clear sections:

• Chapters 1–24 are oracles of judgment against Judah and various strange sign-acts performed by Ezekiel.
• Chapters 25–32 are oracles of judgment against foreign nations and rulers who serve as warnings to Judah.
• Chapters 33–48 are oracles of hope that depict the future restoration of a new and united kingdom and a restored relationship between the people and their God.

In addition to the three major sections of the book, the structure of the narrative tends to focus on four visions:

• In Ezekiel 1:1–3:15, the priest Ezekiel witnesses a vision of the "glory of the LORD" and is commissioned as a prophet to the exilic community.
• Ezekiel 8:1–11:24 sees the prophet transported from Babylon to the city of Jerusalem, where he witnesses abominations committed by the people and sees God's glory depart the temple.

• The "Valley of the Dry Bones" (Ezek 37:1-14) is the most well-known passage from Ezekiel and is a vision of God's people being delivered from their spiritual death and raised to walk in newness of life with God.

• Finally, Ezekiel 40:1–48:35 contains a long and detailed vision of a new temple that brings healing to the land.

Options for Group or Individual Study

It's a lot to ask either individuals or a small group to stick with Ezekiel for one passage, let alone ten. This is not a comprehensive study through all of Ezekiel, and there are some key passages that space has not allowed me to focus on more fully. However, I am hopeful that this book can give you a good glimpse into the nature and character of the God that Ezekiel places before us. For many small groups or Sunday school classes, teachers may want to consider a six-week option to work through Ezekiel rather than the ten-week study presented in this book. If a class or individual wanted to consider a six-week option, this would be my suggestion:

1. Wheels in the Sky (1:1–3:3)
2. The Glory Has Left the Building (10:1–11:25)
3. Sour Grapes (18:1-32)
4. A Heart Transplant (36:16-38)
5. Sticks and Bones (37:1-28)
6. The Lord Is There (40:1-4; 43:1-12; 47:1-12; 48:30-35)

A Transforming Fire

More than anything, I hope you see that Ezekiel is essentially a prophet of hopeful imagination, but it is not cheap hope that comes without experiences of loss and affliction. Instead, it is the hope that believes God can lead the people to green pastures for their souls (34:11-31), the hope that believes God's spirit can infuse people with new life (37:1-14), the hope that believes God can bring unity to a people's entrenched divisions (37:15-28), and the hope that looks for the love of God to flood our world (47:1-12). As you wrestle with what you find in the remarkable book of Ezekiel, allow this bold prophet's radical hope to be an all-consuming fire. It will not destroy you; instead, it will leave you changed, transformed, and redeemed.

Wheels in the Sky

Ezekiel 1:1–3:3

"Christian Leaders: You were trained for a world that is disappearing."

—Tod Bolsinger, *Canoeing the Mountains* (18)

A Thirty-year-old Priest (1:1-3)

For my thirtieth birthday, my wife conspired with my parents to throw me a surprise party. Familiar faces from high school, college, and my current congregation all gathered in my parents' living room. I felt loved and celebrated. Poor Ezekiel did not feel the same way on his thirtieth birthday. He spent his birthday not at a party but at a riverside. He was watching the churning water of the River Chebar in the land of Babylon. No doubt he was recounting all the events in his own life and in the life of his people that had led him to this moment.

Ezekiel is an oddity in the Bible in that it is one of the few books that gives us the exact dates for certain events. We are told that Ezekiel was standing by the riverside "in the thirtieth year, in the fourth month, on the fifth day of the month" (v. 1). Using the Jewish calendar, we can pinpoint this day to July 31, 593 BCE. That may seem like a superfluous detail, but it's important for understanding the nature of this mysterious book.

Many scholars believe that when we are told that the book of Ezekiel begins "in the thirtieth year," it is referring not just to a date but also to Ezekiel's age. That's important because we also learn from this introduction that Ezekiel was from a priestly family. Priests began their term of service near the age of thirty. Interestingly, we shall see that the book of Ezekiel ends exactly twenty years later, when Ezekiel would be fifty, the exact age when priests ended their term of service in the Jerusalem temple. If Ezekiel had remained in Jerusalem, he would have begun his ministry career at the temple. Instead, the temple had been ransacked, and he, along with his family, had been carried off to exile in Babylon.

What we can see from these first three verses is that we are going to encounter a man who thought he would head into ministry in a certain kind of culture. Yet, through circumstances outside his control, he can no longer serve with the stability and predictability he expected. Instead, he now will be called to serve in a new way. Reflecting on the two bookend dates of Ezekiel, Margaret Odell tells us, "The two dates thus suggest that the book presents a memoir of the career of a priest turned prophet" (16).

As this priest-about-to-turn-prophet stared at the river, we are told that "the word of the LORD" came to him and that the "hand of the LORD was on him" (v. 3). Throughout the prophetic texts of the Old Testament, we find examples of both women and men who had abnormal experiences that defy conventional logic. The conclusion is that this vision could only have come from God. As we shall see, this is a vision of hope for a hurting people that is given to a man trying to figure out how to represent God in a changed cultural context.

Those of us who seek to lead in some capacity of Christian ministry in the twenty-first century face a similar dilemma. Our culture has shifted; churches are no longer the locus of public life, religious perspective no longer carries the weight it used to, and droves of people are no longer committing to becoming members of an organized community of faith. Perhaps Ezekiel can serve as a model for us as we seek to discern a new kind of calling in a changed landscape.

Tod Bolsinger has written a book on adaptive Christian leadership called *Canoeing the Mountains*. The title comes from the Lewis and Clark expedition's attempts to map out North America from the Atlantic to the Pacific Ocean. The explorers mistakenly assumed that they would find a riverway that would carry them all the way to the Pacific and prepared for their trip with the supplies for that journey. However, something stood in their way: the Rocky Mountains! Likewise, leadership requires adaptive abilities that are beyond what you have prepared for. Today's ministers and congregational leaders are attempting to guide their churches through changes that nobody could have seen coming a generation ago. Ezekiel anticipated serving as a priest in Jerusalem, but he finds himself by a riverside in Babylon. Such is the way of leadership. Bolsinger writes, "Adaptive capacity is the crucial leadership element for a changing world. . . . This capacity building is more than just some techniques to master. It's a set of deeply developed capabilities that are the result of ongoing transformation in the life of a leader" (90–91).

Four Living Creatures (1:4-14)

As Ezekiel stood by that riverside, contemplating all that his people had been through, he began to see a storm brewing on the horizon. Growing up in southeast Missouri, I was always on the lookout for foreboding gray columns of cloud that could develop into destructive tornadoes. Likewise, Ezekiel may have thought he was seeing a normal thunderstorm forming on the Mesopotamian plain. But as this storm approached, he began to realize that these were no ordinary clouds. This was not meteorology; this was theology. As Ezekiel begins to describe all that he sees in this vision, the Hebrew of the passage is written in an erratic and garbled way. It is almost as if Ezekiel is so moved by this scene that he can't help writing it down in broken speech (Block 1997, 90–91).

In the center of these theological clouds are four bizarre and mysterious creatures. Their bodies are humanlike, but they also have four wings. Their feet are like a calf's and seem to be metallic. Attached to their bodies and under their wings are human hands. In the Bible, imagery of hands often serves as a symbol for power and competence (C. Wright 2001, 48).

Piling onto the strangeness, each of these creatures has four faces: a lion, an eagle, an ox, and a human. Theories abound about the meanings of these symbols. Some scholars believe they correlate to constellations in the nighttime sky, and others believe they are symbols of Babylonian deities, which this vision makes subservient to YHWH (the Lord). In later Christian tradition, the four faces of the living creatures became icons that were associated with the four Gospels in the New Testament; Matthew was the human, Mark was the lion, Luke was the bull, and John was the eagle (Bowen, 5). However, in Ezekiel's context, these creatures would likely have had deep meanings for the exiles. Each of them carries special significance and meaning:

• The *lion* was a symbol of strength and courage (think of the poor lion in the *Wizard of Oz* who had lost his courage!). In cultures all over the ancient Near East, the lion was also a symbol of royalty. Perhaps we could think of the lion as *the greatest of wild land animals.*

• There is a reason that the *eagle* is the national symbol of the United States of America (although Benjamin Franklin lobbied for the turkey!): the eagle is a symbol of swiftness and considered the stateliest of birds. Let us think of the eagle as *the greatest of all flying animals.*

• For people of the ancient Near East, likely the most powerful animal they would ever encounter was the *ox.* It was a symbol of fertility and was the most valuable and useful of all domesticated animals. The ox was *the greatest of all domestic animals.*

• Finally, there is the *human being.* While we often fail to live up to this ideal, the human being serves a symbol for *the most noble of all creatures.*

The choice of these four faces on the creatures whose sole purpose is to worship God serves as a symbol for the universal sovereignty of God over all of creation. As magnificent as these four-faced, divine creatures are, they serve only as the warm-up act for God's appearance in Ezekiel's vision. The purpose of all beasts of the field, all birds of the air, all animals on a farm, and all human beings is to worship their Creator:

> All creatures of our God and King,
> lift up your voice and with us sing
> Alleluia, alleluia!

Wheels within Wheels (1:15-21)

No other image in Ezekiel's inaugural vision has caused as much wild speculation as the images of the "wheels within wheels" in verses 15-21. In the 1970s, when there was increased interest in the existence of extraterrestrial life, numerous books were published that claimed Ezekiel had seen UFOs in his vision. The true purpose of these wheels, however, is to serve as an image that captures God's omnipresence (God is everywhere) and omniscience (God knows all things).

It's best to imagine the wheels as two wheels that intersect with one another at a right angle. The point of the wheel-within-a-wheel is that these wheels can move forward and backward as well as side to side. As the four living creatures prepare the way for the one on the throne, they move the wheels in any direction. Furthermore, we read that the wheels are made of precious metals and contain eyeballs along the rim. In biblical imagery, eyes are signs of knowledge and awareness. These are strange wheels, indeed, but their description here is not just a journalistic report; it is meant to teach us about who God is.

The final detail we are given about these wheels is that they do not move on their own. Instead, they are guided by "the spirit of the living creatures" (v. 20). The Hebrew word here for "spirit" is the word *ruah*, and it will be an important word for our exploration of Ezekiel. This Hebrew word can be translated as "spirit," "wind," or "breath." Ezekiel is often called the "prophet of the spirit" due to the number of times he uses this word (Block 1997, 101). We learn here that the movement of the wheels is not arbitrary but is intentional and guided.

Imagine that you are an ancient Israelite whose faith has been closely tied to the location of the temple in Jerusalem. Now you are exiled in Babylon and cut off from your beloved house of worship in your home city. Perhaps you are wrestling with the question, "Can God hear my prayers in Babylon? Will God be present with me during exile in this foreign land?" The wheels are a sign of comfort that yes, the God of Abraham, Isaac, and Jacob will always be able to be present with God's people because this God is a mobile God!

A Dome and a Throne (1:22-28)

Swirling above the heads of the four living creatures and the wheels-within-wheels is a shiny firmament or a dome. We will soon learn that this dome serves as a boundary that separates the living creatures from the one seated on the throne. Remember that this vision is not just a journalistic description of a cosmic vision; this vision's primary purpose is theology—to teach us about God. The dome separates the living creatures from God because Ezekiel wants to make it clear that as majestic as these angelic beings may appear, they are ultimately subservient to and separate from God. In Genesis 1, God's act of creation is to bring order out of chaos by separating the heavenly from the earthly (Odell, 29–30). This dome helps to make it abundantly clear that there is a difference between creation and the Creator.

Ezekiel's perspective continues to pan upwards until we see a heavenly throne with an occupant described as "something that seemed like a human form" (v. 26). The throne itself is made of lapis lazuli, one of the rarest and most precious stones known in the ancient world (Block 1997, 104). Emanating from the throne and the human figure atop it is the most elaborate and colorful show one could imagine. Ezekiel describes it as being surrounded by a rainbow.

The realization of what he is seeing and experiencing slowly begins to dawn on Ezekiel. Perhaps he initially wonders if he is seeing a vision from the pantheon of gods in Babylon. But no, that can't be right. As Christopher Wright puts it,

> This is no Babylonian deity attended by its guardian sphinxes. This is none other than Yahweh himself, very much alive and well and still on the throne. *Yahweh* is here in Babylon! The shock of the realization drains the last dregs of adrenalin from Ezekiel's trembling body and he collapses *face down*, unable to look any longer. (2001, 51)

Ezekiel is so overcome by this awe-inducing, fantastical image before him that he can only bring himself to refer to this vision as "the appearance of the likeness of the glory of the LORD" (v. 28).

A Scroll: It's What's for Dinner (2:1–3:3)

As if the visuals were not enough, Ezekiel then hears the voice of the one seated on the throne speaking to him. It calls him to stand on his feet, and when he has done so a spirit (*ruah*) enters him. We again encounter the dynamic Hebrew word *ruah*. This word can hold a multiplicity of meanings, and those meanings are manifest in the calling of Ezekiel. This man is now breathed on by the Almighty. Ezekiel's calling is to be a prophet to a people who are rebellious, stubborn, and spiritually deaf (from God's perspective). Ezekiel is warned that their negativity is contagious; he is to take great care that he does not wallow in the muck of their pessimism or disobedience. Instead, Ezekiel is to remain a differentiated presence who refuses to engage in the community's game of weaseling out of their covenantal fidelity to God.

The one seated on the throne then leans forward to offer Ezekiel a scroll. Ezekiel takes the scroll and eats it. For a man trained for the service of the temple priesthood, any purposeful destruction of the written word was likely a hard-to-swallow request. We will see throughout Ezekiel that he is asked to physically embody the messages he receives from God. Ezekiel obeys and consumes the scroll. He is not simply to nibble at the scroll, but God commands him to cram it in and "fill your stomach with it" (3:3). Though the scroll is full of words of lament and woe, the taste of the words is sweet in Ezekiel's mouth. Perhaps the sweetness is God's act of grace to comfort Ezekiel before he is to deliver such sobering and harsh words to the people ("a spoonful of sugar helps the medicine go down"). Or perhaps the sweetness derives from the divine intentions of the words of judgment and woe. Are these words harrowing and difficult when first received? Yes, of course. But on the other side is hope and restoration. What Ezekiel (and we who journey with him) will find is that even out of the bitter ashes of exile and despair comes the sweetness of new life and resurrection.

Conclusion

In her novel *The Dearly Beloved*, Cara Wall tells the story of two young ministers who co-pastor a small congregation in 1960s New York City. One of the ministers, James, is married to Nan, who finds herself struggling with some of her life's circumstances. Nan desperately wishes that all the things she longs for were simply provided for her and that God would speak clearly to her. However, James asks her to consider that there may be a great purpose behind her sense of restlessness:

> "Those feelings that hound you, Nan—they are God. They are God telling you to do something, to be different in some way. Sometimes it isn't right to pray for acceptance of the status quo. If God calls you to upend it, then you should upend it. You think God rewards, Nan, I think God pursues." (245)

Ezekiel's story is one of adaptive leadership during rapid change. In this opening vision, he is confronted with the way that the calling on his life is being molded and shaped, not by his own expectations, but by the sovereignty of God. Our divine callings are not the products of our wish-list expectations of what we want out of life; they are the ways that God has equipped us to meet the moment in which we are born. Ezekiel thought he would minister to God's people with priestly accoutrements as he spoke the words of Torah over the temple sacrifices. Instead, he is told to eat and embody those very words by a Babylonian riverside. Even in exile, Ezekiel has found himself pursued by the glory of God.

1. When have you had to adapt your assumptions because of a change in your circumstances?

_____

_____

_____

_____

_____

2. Finish this statement: "I am called to _____."

_____

_____

_____

_____

_____

3. What do you think are some of the challenges facing churches and congregational leaders today?

_____

_____

_____

_____

_____

4. What is an experience you have had in nature that has deeply moved you?

_____

_____

_____

_____

_____

5. *New Testament Connection:* Read Revelation 4:1-11. Why do you think John's vision and Ezekiel's vision of the four living creatures share so many similarities?

_____

_____

_____

_____

_____

6. Do you associate God's presence with a certain place? If so, where?

_____

_____

_____

_____

_____

7. *New Testament Connection:* Read Revelation 10:8-11. Compare and contrast Ezekiel's and John's experiences with being commanded to consume a scroll.

_____

_____

_____

_____

_____

8. What is a meaningful experience that you have had during worship? How did that experience change you?

_____

_____

_____

_____

_____

9. Ezekiel has nothing but metaphoric language to describe what he is seeing; it is beyond words. What metaphors for God do you especially connect with in your spirituality?

_____

_____

_____

_____

_____

10. What does it mean for your life that God is shown to be present with the Babylonian exiles?

_____

_____

_____

_____

_____

Street Theater

"All our hurts are held in community. When one member
suffers, all suffer together. The truth is that hope is open
and the world is not closed. The world is indeed fatigued
waiting for governments and armies to devise peace. The
truth is, peace cannot be devised. It can only be permitted
where the truth is told about hurt and hope."

—Walter Brueggemann,
"Reflections on Ezekiel" (96–98)

After his experience of being called by the riverside, Ezekiel hears
directly from God (2:1-10), who tells him that his new vocation is
to deliver a message to God's people. He is warned that his words
will not always be well received and that he should be prepared
for some resistance and sabotage. As a symbol that he carries the
word of the Lord within himself, Ezekiel is instructed to eat a scroll
(3:1-3). From now on, he carries God's word within him, and as we
shall see, his entire life now is devoted to speaking on God's behalf
to the people. Ezekiel is then carried away and placed in the midst
of the exiles, where he is so stunned by his visionary experiences that
he does not speak for seven days (3:12-15).

Who Watches the Watchmen? (3:16-21)

Seven days of stunned silence provide Ezekiel opportunity for reflection on his new calling. In the Bible, seven days also serves as the
appropriate time of mourning a loss (see Job 2:13), and Ezekiel may
be mourning the loss of his anticipated future as a temple priest
while he comes to term with his new calling as a prophet to the
exiles (Bowen, 15). Perhaps God answers this confusion by offering

a metaphor that further illumines his new role: Ezekiel is to serve as a watchman on the wall. In the ancient Near East, cities had sentries whose job was to watch for approaching enemy armies. If they spotted any looming threat, they were to warn the citizens. Likewise, Ezekiel is to convey to the people that God does not take their sin lightly.

Being a watchman was a difficult task for Ezekiel, and it remains a difficult task for today's ministry leaders. The gospel is the ultimate good news, but it does contain dire warnings about the consequences of unbridled individualism and of communal negligence of justice. After all, as the Apostle Paul writes, "the wages of sin is death" (Rom 6:23). Speaking about sin and brokenness in today's culture will not garner a preacher worldly popularity, but it is a vital part of the responsibility to speak on God's behalf.

This image of being a watchman is not without a dose of hope for Ezekiel. It's also a role that clearly had staying power for Ezekiel; he will return to the metaphor in Ezekiel 33:1-9. God affirms that Ezekiel will not be held accountable for how the people respond to his proclamations. Instead, God cares only that Ezekiel is faithful as a proclaimer. As Daniel Block says, "The prophet's call is not 'to save souls' (which is God's affair), but to proclaim the message he receives from the divine Commissioner. Faithfulness in service is measured not by effectiveness but by fidelity to the divine charge" (1997, 150).

A Strange Homecoming (3:22-27)

After Ezekiel receives his commission as a watchman to the people, the text takes one of the strangest and most paradoxical turns in the Bible. Ezekiel again encounters the glory (*kabod*) of God and recognizes it as the same vision he experienced at the River Chebar. Perhaps he has prepared himself to hear about what he is supposed to preach to the people. Maybe Ezekiel said, "OK. I'm ready, Lord. Tell me what I'm supposed to say on your behalf." And what is God's grand message for Ezekiel? God tells him to go back to his house, to allow himself to be tied up with ropes, and that God will make his tongue cling to the roof of his mouth so that he is unable to speak. We can imagine Ezekiel responding with a dumbfounded, "Wait . . . what?" How is one supposed to be a sentry on the wall if they are shut in their house, tied up, and unable to speak?

The answer lies in the fact that Ezekiel is not called to be an ordinary prophet (just as he had to realize that he would not be serving as an ordinary priest). Instead, this passage is the first of

Ezekiel's "sign-acts." Throughout the book of Ezekiel, we will see him being asked to embody numerous messages in a form of street theater. Just as dancing can communicate ideas that mere words cannot, these sign-acts preach more boldly than any simple sermon. However, they often come at great cost to Ezekiel.

Ezekiel is likely being bound with ropes to demonstrate the position of God's people in exile. They are bound by their experience of exile and are seemingly unable to move beyond their present circumstances. Specifically, the Hebrew word for the ropes used to bind Ezekiel is 'abotim. This term is specifically used when talking about the garments worn by priests in the book of Exodus (Odell, 57). This is yet another example of Ezekiel's vocational expectations being adapted for the culture of exile; he is receiving some of the priestly initiations, but in a way that affirms his adapted job as an exilic prophet.

Toy Story (4:1-3)

Ezekiel then performs another sign-act that this time portrays God's perspective on what has happened to the city of Jerusalem. The prophet takes a brick that is still soft, wet clay before it is fired in a kiln. On the brick, he draws an outline of the city of Jerusalem. For exiles in Babylon, no doubt that image would have been familiar. Ezekiel then takes some objects and, almost like playing with a bucket of military toys, begins to portray the siege against Jerusalem. Then, with Ezekiel playing the role of God, he sets his own face next to Jerusalem. The image of "the face of God" was a familiar illustration in Israelite theology for God's favor and love (see Num 6:24-26). But then Ezekiel takes an iron griddle and sets it between his face and the brick of Jerusalem. He portrays the heartbreaking truth that, because of the people's lack of fidelity to their covenant, God has hidden God's face from them.

Lying Around (4:4-8)

God then instructs Ezekiel to lie on his left side for 390 days and then to turn and lie on his right side for 40 days. We would not blame Ezekiel if he began to think to himself, "This is not what I signed up for!" (But buckle up, buddy; you aren't done yet.) What is this sign-act supposed to symbolize?

Ezekiel was to lie on his left for 390 days to symbolize the long history of Israel. In this act, each day represents one year. If you were to count backwards from Ezekiel's time, then 390 years in the past would lead you to approximately 982 BCE, which was roughly the time when the Israelite monarchy began. When Ezekiel turns to lie on his right side for 40 days, that symbolizes the experience of the exiles in Babylon. The number 40 and especially the period of 40 years would have immediately called to mind the 40 years their ancestors spent in the wilderness prior to entering the promised land. Through Ezekiel, God is telling the people that their experience in exile will be akin to their ancestors' time in the wilderness. In both cases, those are times of refinement and repentance (Odell, 63).

God tells Ezekiel that his lying on each side for so long is to symbolize that he is to bear the punishment or sin of the people. This serves as yet another connection to the role that Ezekiel thought he would likely play: a priest. The book of Leviticus tells us that the role of the priest in the community was to, at times, represent the sin of the people. For example, in Leviticus 16, the priest was to lay his hands upon a scapegoat in a symbolic transference of the community's sin. Even as he lies there in a sign-act that is no doubt uncomfortable and strange, Ezekiel is demonstrating love for his people in fulfilling his role of speaking on God's behalf. His life itself is now the message.

Organic Bread (4:9-17)

Ezekiel is then instructed to make himself a meal. He is to take wheat, barley, beans, lentils, millet, and spelt and mash them all into a dough. This is to be his food while he lies on his left side. He is also to severely limit his rations to only about eight ounces of food each day and about two-thirds of a liter of water. This amount of food and water would have kept Ezekiel alive, but barely. If that wasn't bad enough, Ezekiel was likely unprepared for the next instructions God gives him on how to cook the bread; he is to bake his bread over human excrement.

The next time you find yourself in a Trader Joe's or an organic food store, you might find a loaf of bread in the freezer section called Ezekiel 4:9 Bread. It is a bread that claims to be made with the six ingredients given to Ezekiel to make his bread. The company seems to take this Scripture literally, so it raises the question, *How exactly do they bake their bread?* Personally, I am fine not knowing that answer.

When Ezekiel hears that he is to bake his bread over human excrement, he objects—the only time in the book of Ezekiel that he does so (Odell, 65). He objects not only because this method of cooking would make his sole source of nourishment ceremonially unclean (see Deut 23:12-14) but also because it would disqualify Ezekiel from serving as a priest to the people. Perhaps Ezekiel was holding on to hope that he could still serve in a ministerial role to his people and was beginning to question the efficacy of these sign-acts. God compromises with Ezekiel and allows him to use cow dung rather than human feces to cook his bread. It would still be unclean, but not quite as disgusting.

Why would God ask this of Ezekiel? The point of this Great Babylonian Bake Off is that Ezekiel is, yet again, embodying the experience of exile. Normally, the six ingredients used to make this bread would never have been put together to make food. Ezekiel is demonstrating the only kind of sustenance that will be available when people are forced to scrape the bottom of all their barrels to make the most meager of foods (Block 1997, 184). Ezekiel is forcing the people to see the effects of violating the covenant by embodying the realities of a besieged people.

In 2002, the Feeding Children Better program developed a series of television commercials to highlight childhood poverty in the United States. In one ad, a woman is seen walking into various fast food restaurants and mall food courts. She approaches the counter of utensils and condiments, and we see her grabbing handfuls of items and stuffing them into the pockets of her coat. She then goes home, where she takes out a number of ketchup packets and sets them on the counter. One by one, she empties the packets into a pot and adds water. She cooks the ketchup soup and serves the meager rations to her three children (see "ConAgra Foods' Feeding Children Better Foundation").

In a way, this is exactly what Ezekiel is doing here. He is forcing his people to confront the realities of poverty and all the forces that converge to force people into it. In the Gospel of Matthew, Jesus Christ reminds his disciples that whenever they encounter the hungry in their own midst, they are to treat them with divine dignity and concern: "for I was hungry and you gave me food, I was thirsty and you gave me something to drink . . ." (Matt 25:35).

A Close Shave (5:1-4)

No doubt emaciated and exhausted from his meager rations, Ezekiel is asked to perform one last sign-act in this series. He is to take a sword and cut off his own hair and beard. Even with a modern, state-of-the-art razor, it is easy to make a mistake while shaving; one can hardly imagine the difficulty of using a dull sword to shave one's head and face.

What was the purpose of this shave? Strange theories, including some with Freudian, psychosexual tones, abound among biblical scholars. However, as Daniel Smith-Christopher says, "When analyzing a refugee's paranoia, surely a sword is sometimes just a sword" (88). Smith-Christopher and others effectively argue that Ezekiel's shaving here is meant to embody the experience of the exilic refugees in numerous ways. First, shaving was prohibited to priests, so this is yet another sign that Ezekiel's own calling and vocation have undergone a terrible transformation in the context of exile. Second, shaving one's head and beard was often a sign of tremendous mourning, and Ezekiel is embodying the heartache and suffering of his people. Third, being shaved was an act of humiliation (remember that the White Witch commands that Aslan the Great Lion be shaved before being executed in C. S. Lewis's *The Lion, the Witch, and the Wardrobe*). As if Ezekiel wasn't already feeling ashamed enough, he now stands before his people gaunt and bald.

Ezekiel then takes his shorn hair and divides it into thirds. With each of the thirds, he commits a public act of demonstration:

- The first third he tosses into the fire. As the sickening smell of burning hair wafts up, the people are reminded of the costs of exile as they realize this first third represents the fate of those left in Jerusalem.
- Ezekiel tosses the second bundle of hair into the air and then chops it up with his sword. This symbolizes the people who have escaped the fires of Jerusalem only to be cut down by an enemy's blade.
- Taking the final third of the hair, Ezekiel tosses it to the wind and watches it scatter. This represents the Diaspora of God's people who no longer have a homeland but are now scattered among the nations of the world (C. Wright 2001, 84–85).
- Finally, Ezekiel gathers some of the remaining strands of hair and begins to weave them into the tassels of his robe.

This is the sad and sorry remnant of God's people. However, let's not gloss over the power of this moment. While being tied up with ropes, being confined to his home, being silent, using miniatures to portray the siege of his beloved city, lying on each side for an inordinate amount of time, eating tasteless and unclean bread, starving himself, and being humiliatingly shaved, Ezekiel's line of sign-acts ends with a flickering flame of hope.

Conclusion

According to the American Psychological Association, narrative exposure therapy (NET) is a treatment meant to help individuals establish a coherent life narrative in which to contextualize traumatic experiences. It is especially known for its uses in group treatment with refugees. The key elements of a therapist who practices NET are compassionate understanding, active listening, therapeutic alliance, and unequivocal positive regard (see APA). I certainly don't think that everything Ezekiel has done in this passage would be approved by modern psychologists. Yet I also think that his strange acts of street theater serve a quasi-therapeutic purpose. For the exiles who have experienced deportation, scarce resources, and the loss of their communal identity, there may be something healing about seeing their experiences embodied in such a visceral way. Perhaps one of the intents of Ezekiel's sign-acts was to demonstrate empathy with the exiles' struggles. Let's not forget that Ezekiel does not act on his own but at the direction of YHWH. So perhaps it is truly God who seeks to connect with the people and even to help them establish a new narrative for their lives.

1. Some Christians want to emphasize grace and ignore sin while others seem to dwell on sin to the detriment of grace. How can we find a healthy balance in how we communicate the gospel?

_____

_____

_____

_____

_____

2. God does not require Ezekiel to be successful but only to be faithful. How are you required to be faithful in your own calling as opposed to merely being successful?

_____

_____

_____

_____

_____

3. Yet again, Ezekiel is faced with the realization that his calling as a priest must be transformed in the face of a rapidly changing world. How can we continue to be flexible in how live out our faith in our own ever-shifting context?

_____

_____

_____

_____

_____

4. Can you think of a leader who seemed to embody the struggles in their community?

_____

_____

_____

_____

_____

5. How do you think you would have responded if you were one of Ezekiel's neighbors watching him perform these various sign-acts?

_____

_____

_____

_____

6. *New Testament Connection:* Read Acts 10:9-16. Compare and contrast Ezekiel's and Peter's experiences.

_____

_____

_____

_____

_____

7. What can you and/or your congregation do to address hunger in your own community? Go to www.feedingamerica.org to learn the startling statistics and some best practices for getting started.

_____

_____

_____

_____

_____

8. Do you think the performance of these sign-acts fostered deeper empathy in Ezekiel?

_____

_____

_____

_____

_____

9. When have you had to cling to a small flickering flame of hope in the midst of overwhelming darkness?

_____

_____

_____

_____

_____

10. Do you see any good news in these passages?

_____

_____

_____

_____

_____

Idol Hands

"There are no unsacred places;
there are only sacred places
and desecrated places."

—Wendell Berry, "How to be a Poet"

We have just seen how Ezekiel embodied the experience of exile. With his street theater of sign-acts, the prophet showed the struggle, the poverty, and the pain that accompanied being separated from the city of Jerusalem and the temple. These sign-acts surely formed within Ezekiel a deeper sense of empathy for the experiences of those suffering the consequences of exile. In our next passage, Ezekiel begins to glimpse and understand the painful experiences of another one whose heart is broken: God.

Whisked Away (8:1-4)

We begin with another exact date. This second vision happens on the fifth day of the sixth month of the sixth year of the exile (September 18, 592 BCE; Odell, 103). It takes place almost fourteen months after Ezekiel's initial vision of God's glory by the River Chebar (see session 1). We find Ezekiel on this September day in his house entertaining guests. He is playing host to the elders of the community. Perhaps they are visiting him to seek an explanation for why he is behaving so strangely (cutting his hair, lying on his side, cooking his bread over dung). However, the elders' visit does show us that Ezekiel still plays a leadership role within the community of exiles. He is serving a priestly role—just not in the way he had expected to.

Their visit is suddenly interrupted by the appearance of a heavenly figure. The figure grabs Ezekiel by the hair and whisks him away to yet another vision involving God's glory, but this time he finds himself at the temple in Jerusalem. After being separated from the temple, Ezekiel may have been delighted to find himself in that sacred space. However, he quickly discovers that all is not right at the temple. This sacred space has become a place of desecration and idolatry.

It begins with Ezekiel noticing a statue at the entrance of the temple's inner sanctuary. He calls this statue *haqqina hammaqneh*, a singsong term that is literally translated "the jealousy that provokes jealousy" (Block 1997, 282). It's no doubt called this because of the emotions it stirs within the heart of God: "For you shall worship no other god, because the LORD, whose name is Jealous, is a jealous God" (Exod 34:14). The presence of this jealousy-inducing statue is our first sign that all is not right at God's temple. This statue is an affront and insult to God's glory.

Four scenes follow that show the depth of idolatry that has infected the culture of the temple in Jerusalem. These actions clearly have broken the heart of the covenantal God who asks for relational fidelity from God's people.

Scene 1: The Jealousy that Provokes Jealousy (8:5-6)

In the first scene, God gives Ezekiel a closer look at the statue, the *haqqina hammaqneh*, that has been erected at the entrance of the temple's inner sanctuary. We already know the presence of this statue has brought forth feelings of jealousy within God, but we are not given a great deal of clues as to the specifics of this statue. Likely, it is a statue to the goddess Asherah, a consort of the Canaanite god Baal (C. Wright 2001, 100). The Israelites had been tempted in the past to syncretize their covenantal faith with the beliefs of surrounding cultures. Past regimes had erected statues of Asherah in the temple, but they were removed during the reforms of King Josiah (see 2 Kings 21:7, 23:6).

It is not merely the presence of the statue that infuriates God. It is also the fact that the people are committing "great abominations" (v. 6) before the statue. Ancient sources tell us that some of the worship practices surrounding Asherah involved fertility rituals and sexual practices that would have been against the covenantal regulations in the Torah (C. Wright 2001, 101). In other words, God's hatred for this statue is not merely because of the statue being present in the temple; it is because the people have allowed their behavior to be formed by another way of being. This way invades and infringes on God's sovereignty.

Scene 2: Animal House (8:7-13)

Ezekiel is then taken to a portion of the temple entrance that has a hole in the wall. Ezekiel digs through the hole and comes upon an entrance to an inner room. What is the meaning of Ezekiel completing this hole in the wall? Theories abound, but one detail that may help shed some light is the fact that Ezekiel has been taken "to the entrance of the gateway of the inner court that faces north" (v. 3). Later in the Old Testament, when Nehemiah is assessing the damage done to the walls of the city during the Babylonian siege, he asks for the majority of the workers to fix the walls facing north (see Neh 2:11-20). Ostensibly that would imply that the northern walls bore the brunt of the destruction brought by the Babylonian army. Ezekiel is likely creating a hole in this northern wall of the temple to signify the battering rams that will crash through the walls of the city of Jerusalem (Smith-Christopher, 87–88).

When he comes through the wall, Ezekiel encounters a room adorned with the images of all kinds of animals. The animals on the walls are repulsive to Ezekiel. They are clearly the sort of unclean creatures avoided in Israelite theology such as crocodiles, ostriches, snakes, and cockroaches (see Lev 11:1-47). Ezekiel sees some of the contemporary civic and political leaders of his day burning incense in homage to the animals.

Some scholars recognize political motivations behind these civic leaders' actions. The sort of animals described here were highly revered and worshiped in Egypt. The elders of Israel justify their worship of these animals by saying that God has abandoned them. The civic leaders hope that appealing to foreign gods will help them win the favor of the Egyptian deities. In the past, King Jehoiakim had relied on the military might of Egypt, and it is likely that Egyptian totems of worship were brought to Jerusalem (Jenson, 80).

These elders in the temple have chosen to replace the sovereignty of God with Egypt's idols of political power and military might. Old Testament scholar Christopher Wright has written a book on idolatry called *"Here Are Your Gods": Faithful Discipleship in Idolatrous Times*. He writes about the modern-day temptations to commit idolatry that churches in the West continue to face today, including that of politics and militarism. He writes, "It is not just that we have begun to mimic nations that engage in spectacularly boastful displays of military hardware and massed human forces. It is the willingness of Christian churches to seemingly sanctify and baptize emblems of national pride and the military virulence of the state that I find syncretistic" (C. Wright 2020, 99).

Scene 3: Weeping for Tammuz (8:14-15)

The next scene Ezekiel witnesses is of a group of women mourning and wailing for a being called Tammuz. This is the only reference to Tammuz in the Hebrew Bible, but the ancient Sumerian writings tell us the Babylonians believed Tammuz was a shepherd-king who ruled for 36,000 years. He was associated with agricultural cycles in the world, and the women may be mourning his loss in the hopes that their land will experience agricultural favor. But the most insidious part of this idolatry is that the women are lamenting a being who is dead while they are in the temple of the living God (Block 1997, 296).

Rather than looking toward the future or being aware of God in the present, these women are obsessed with the past. There is a temptation to make the past into an idol. We can pine for "good old days" to such an extent that we are blind to what is happening here and now. People of Christian faith know well that our belief spurs us to look at right now rather than at the past: "Why do you look for the living among the dead? He is not here, but has risen" (Luke 24:5).

Scene 4: The Sun and the Moon (8:16-18)

For the concluding act of idolatry, Ezekiel is brought to the inner court of the temple. Throughout chapter 8, we have moved more and more toward the interior of this sacred space. Now we will witness that spiritual rot has spread to the very core.

Ezekiel sees twenty-five men who are prostrating themselves before the sun. Astral worship was common in the ancient Near East, but the Hebrew Bible maintains that these creations are not worthy of worship. The sun was also among the most powerful deities in Babylonian cosmology. Likely these men are appealing to the gods of Babylon in the hopes that they will garner favor and save Jerusalem from the wrath of the empire (C. Wright 2001, 108). This yet another example of political idolatry; the men are placing their hopes in other gods and the militaristic powers that serve them, yet they are facing away from the temple of the living God.

There is a great deal of visual, dark humor in this scene. The men prostrate themselves before the sun with their backs to the temple. This means the sun is literally illuminating the temple behind them. It's almost as if God is trying to point out to them where their worship and allegiance truly belong. God is clearly offended at this behavior and turns to Ezekiel to say, "Have you seen this? Can you believe these people?" Then God says something strange: "See, they are putting the branch to their nose!" (v. 17), which literally translates as *sticking the branch up my nose*, meaning God's nose. Biblical scholars are not sure what to make of this. It's possible that the phrase is an ancient idiom that stands in for an insult (Block 1997, 299). But the Hebrew word for "branch" is similar to the Hebrew for "bad smell." Perhaps Ezekiel witnesses an embarrassing scene like the one Robert Jenson describes: "In a large group of persons repeatedly prostrating themselves, unfortunate digestive events may occur, which since these priests were facing away from the most holy place, would indeed have been right in the Lord's nose" (81).

God's heart is utterly broken by these acts of idolatry. God has taken Ezekiel from the land of Babylon back to Jerusalem to show Ezekiel the extent of the people's infidelity to their covenant with God. And these idolatrous acts have heartbreaking consequences. In verse 17, God laments that they are filling "the land with violence." When the people adopt the theological perspective of the empire, they begin to embody the ethics of the empire. This leads to an increase in harmful nationalism, reliant militarism, and violence against the poor and marginalized in their midst. These acts of idolatry have provoked God's anger and wrath. In Ezekiel 9:1-11, we read of a vision in which God executes all of those in Israel who have willingly committed these egregious acts.

Conclusion

In the twenty-first century, we may not struggle with worshiping animals, dead deities, or the sun, but idolatry remains an ever-present reality. In the evangelical church I grew up in, I remember our Sunday school classes occasionally spending time exploring the beliefs of other religions. Our teacher would usually call these "cults," and we would marvel at how people could be so bamboozled by these odd and foreign beliefs. We would be warned to remain faithful to Jesus and not be swayed by the "idolatry" of other religions. However, Ezekiel 8 demonstrates that the source of idolatry is not found in the world but within our own hearts. The source of the people's idolatry came not from imposition by foreign powers but by their willing acceptance of worshiping other gods, including the political symbols of the empire.

The book of Revelation is about the people of God being encouraged to persevere (Gk., *hypomone*) in their worship of God and God alone amid the temptations to succumb to the imperial cult of the Roman Empire. This is no less a temptation in our time. God's heart desires a people who will persevere in their covenantal fidelity to worship and glorify God and God alone.

1. Why do you think God wanted Ezekiel to witness what was taking place in the temple in Jerusalem?

_____

_____

_____

_____

_____

2. For many modern readers, the concept of idolatry may seem archaic and outdated. But how do you see idolatry being practiced in our world today?

_____

_____

_____

_____

_____

3. What do you make of the Old Testament passage that tells us God is prone to jealousy? How does that make you feel, and how should that change our behavior?

_____

_____

_____

_____

_____

4. In scene 1, the people place their faith in the Babylonian goddess Asherah. Why do you think Israelites who remained in Jerusalem were tempted to worship a Babylonian deity?

_____

_____

_____

_____

_____

5. Scene 2 depicts civic leaders appealing to the might of the Egyptian army. In our modern world, where do you see people appealing to military might in unhealthy ways?

_____

_____

_____

_____

6. When we come to scene 3, we encounter women weeping for a mythical figure in the past. What is tempting about worshiping the past?

_____

_____

_____

_____

_____

7. Scene 4 is a jarring scene in that these priests are bowing down to the sun. How do you we seek to care for creation without worshiping creation itself?

_____

_____

_____

_____

8. Remember that Ezekiel comes from one exilic perspective. How might the Israelites left in Jerusalem have seen these actions differently?

_____

_____

_____

_____

_____

9. _New Testament Connection:_ **Read Luke 4:1-13. What are the ways that Satan attempts to cause Jesus to commit idolatry?**

_____

_____

_____

_____

_____

10. How are God's people called to persevere (Gk., _hypomone_**) in our own culture?**

_____

_____

_____

_____

_____

4

The Glory Has
Left the Building

Ezekiel 10:1–11:25

"Never forget that justice is what love looks like in public."
—Cornel West, "Askwith Forum"

Chapters 8–11 of Ezekiel are one long vision often called the first of Ezekiel's "Temple Visions." In the previous lesson on chapter 8, we saw how Ezekiel witnessed acts of idolatry within the temple of God, and Ezekiel 9 is a violent depiction of the idolaters being executed for defiling the temple. From our twenty-first-century perspective, these stories of slaughter can leave us feeling squeamish (as well they should). But Ezekiel and the other prophets were reaching for top-shelf metaphors to truly hammer home the message of how seriously God takes our holiness and our worship. And as this "Temple Vision" continues into chapters 10–11, we see Ezekiel's tour of Jerusalem taking him from the temple and into the city itself. We see that the fruit of idolatry is political corruption, narcissistic leaders, and social injustice.

Burning Coals (10:1-17)

As Ezekiel's vision at the temple continues, we find some images we have already encountered—the heavenly throne with its wheels-within-wheels and four living creatures. Collectively, these symbols form what Ezekiel refers to as God's glory. The Hebrew word used for "glory" is *kabod* and can be translated as "glory, esteem, and reputation." These symbols that we have seen since Ezekiel's inaugural vision in chapter 1 represent the nature and character of the holy God. And as Ezekiel's vision in chapter 10 begins, this glory is floating above the place where Israelites assumed it traditionally belonged: God's temple.

However, a strange instruction is given to the "man clothed in linen" (v. 2). Linen was the fabric traditionally used by priests; this character seems to be a combination of an angelic messenger and a high priest (Block 1997, 304–305). Since Ezekiel has just seen a vision of the temple full of idolatry (ch. 8), perhaps this "man clothed in linen" is meant to play the role of a priest because the priests in the temple have failed so miserably. This angel-priest in linen is told to remove burning coals from the four living creatures and from the wheels-within-wheels, and he is to scatter these flaming rocks throughout the city.

In the Bible, fire is usually a sign of God's judgment and wrath. Most often it is used as an image against Israel's enemies (see Ps 97:3; Isa 26:11), but here it is God's own people who are receiving the fire. The anger of God kindled by the scenes of idolatry in the temple is now spreading throughout the city.

The Glory Leaves the Temple (10:18-22)

God's glory then seems to decide that it has finally had enough and begins to leave the temple. The glory leaves the inner area of the temple and departs to the east gate, where it rests. Notice how Ezekiel refers to the temple in verse 18: "the house." Because God has been alienated from the temple, it is now referred to in impersonal and distant terms (Block 1997, 326). Worship is fundamentally a human response to God. When humans no longer acknowledge or seek out the ways that God has already moved and worked among them, worship ceases. What is clear from Ezekiel is that God, with deep *pathos*, has felt ignored and abandoned in the temple. It is now a shell of its former self. It is no longer God's house; it is simply "the house."

The Fruit of Idolatry: Corrupt Leadership (11:1-13)

As God's glory floats above the east gate of the temple, God's spirit lifts Ezekiel himself there so that he may witness a scene taking place. Two political leaders in Jerusalem are patting themselves on the back with the self-assurance that they have everything under control. The names of the two leaders are brimming with irony: Pelatiah means "God has rescued" and Benaiah means "God has built" (Block 1997, 331). Their very names attest to the salvific and generative power of God, yet they are bragging about their own virtues as civic leaders.

Their boasting takes the form of a metaphor. They say to one another, "Gentlemen, this city is an iron pot and we are the meat that give the stew its flavor." This image of a pot (which Ezekiel will later take up himself in ch. 24) is meant to convey that the leaders believe the city is like a shut-tight, thick-walled crock. They are placing their faith in their own ability to provide security for their city. They are placing their faith in their own ability to provide security for their city. And they see themselves not simply as stew meat but as prime, expensive cuts of meat. The Hebrew word that these leaders use for themselves when they say they are the "meat" is a term referring to the best-of-the-best slices of meat (Block 1997, 333–34). In their eyes, they are the cream of the crop. As the leaders who have remained in Jerusalem, they are likely comparing themselves to the exiled. These leaders say to themselves, "God must have really hated those exiles to have allowed them to be carried off like that. Who needs them? We are here and we are the leaders God really wants to be in charge. We are doing such a good job!" If Twitter had been around, how much do you want to bet that they would have tweeted these things about themselves?

However, God points out to Ezekiel that these boastful leaders are kidding themselves. They are not doing a good job of leading the city because they have allowed rampant injustice to infest Jerusalem. God complains against the leaders and says, "You have killed many in this city, and have filled its streets with the slain" (v. 6). These leaders, it turns out, have blood on their hands. The Hebrew word used for the slain here is *halalim*, and it can refer to two different kinds of victims: those who have fallen in battle and those who have been sentenced to death by corrupt courts (Block 1997, 335). Pelatiah, Benaiah, and their entourage are not wise counselors; they are butchers. God takes their metaphorical bragging and says, "You're exactly right. This city is a pot, but the meat filling it is the victims of the systems of injustice you have created."

These systems of injustice perpetuated by the leaders cannot be separated from the acts of idolatry we read about in Ezekiel 8. Injustice and idolatry are always connected. Idolatry is when we separate ourselves from the worship of God and begin to believe that we know better than God. This sort of self-serving thinking always leads to injustice, both on an individual and communal level. In an essay for Good Faith Media titled "Injustice and Idolatry," Baptist professor of religion Colin Harris writes about the Old Testament prophetic tradition of combating injustice by bringing God's people back to faithful, covenantal fidelity. Without that faithfulness, people seek to legitimize the status quo (especially those whose pockets will be lined). Harris writes, "When the systematic injustice that is part of a society's structure and normal practice is challenged, the defensive response of those who benefit from it is often clothed in a religious mantle that claims divine sanction for the way things are."

After turning the metaphorical tables on these leaders, Ezekiel is taken aback when Pelatiah suddenly dies. The one whose name means "God has rescued" now has experienced the wrath of that very God. This creates an emotional response in Ezekiel, who cries out to God, "Is anybody going to be left in Israel?" God answers that question in the next scene of the vision.

Hope for Exiles (11:14-21)

While God indicts the actions of the leaders of the remnant in Israel, God now speaks words of hope to the exiles in Babylon. The hopelessness of the exiles largely rested on the idea that they continued to connect the presence of Yahweh with the temple and the land of Jerusalem. This idea has a long history in the Old Testament. But here, in a revolutionary act of grace, God says, "I will now be their sanctuary" (see v. 16). This idea is without parallel in the entire Old Testament. And it is even more striking that the recipient of this message is Ezekiel himself. Ezekiel, whom we know has deep family ties to the temple, is now the one entrusted with the message that relationship with Yahweh need no longer be tied to the temple. It is worth noting that this theological statement in Ezekiel is not communicating that the temple is now worthless; instead, God is graciously making God's self available to the exiles as a substitute for the temple (Blenkinsopp, 63–64). Ezekiel still dreams of a day when he may serve as a priest in God's temple and when the true glory and purpose of the temple will be restored (see chs. 40–48).

Yet a deeper change must take place within the exiles to make spiritual room for this altered relationship with God. A heart transplant of sorts is required. The idea of gaining a new heart is found elsewhere in Ezekiel (see 18:30-32; 36:22-32). However, whereas elsewhere the promise speaks of a "new heart," the promise here in Ezekiel 11 is of "one heart" (v. 19). The promise of "one heart" to the exiles is a divine gift of unity that will bring together the exilic community (Odell, 124). God is promising to heal communal rifts that may have developed among this stressed and marginalized population. In the midst of his long and final prayer before he is crucified, Jesus in the Gospel of John prays over his disciples and over all of us who will learn from the disciples, "I ask not only on behalf of these, but also on behalf of those who will believe in me through their word, that they all may be one" (John 17:20-21).

The Glory Leaves the City (11:22-25)

After witnessing all of the idolatrous atrocities in the temple and the narcissistic leadership of the city, God's glory has had enough. Having moved from the center of the temple to the east gate, God's glory now moves even farther: to a mountaintop east of the city. God's glory will not be seen in Ezekiel until twenty years later (43:1-4). These intervening years of Ezekiel's ministry will be marked by an absence of God for the people. In addition to God's glory moving to the mountaintop, the Spirit of God now sends Ezekiel all the way back to Babylon, where he delivers a report of this strange prophetic vision to the exiles.

Conclusion

These prophetic visions can make us squirm. And they certainly cause some people to decide that faith simply isn't for them. There is a scene from *The West Wing* where a friend is confiding to President Bartlet that he no longer has faith because he cannot believe that a good God would call for death as a punishment for things such as working on the Sabbath or committing adultery. Bartlet smiles and says, "I'm more of a New Testament man, myself." Most of us can probably relate to Bartlet and simply ignore these old texts in lieu of what we consider to be the more peaceable New Testament.

However, these texts contain strong indictments to remind us that God does not take sin or injustice lightly. The New Testament does not change that. As we can see from this vision in Ezekiel 11, the origin of injustice in our world is essentially idolatry. As we look at systemic racism in our culture, the origin is a lack of recognizing the *Imago Dei* ("the image of God") in each human being. The origin of our conflicts over immigration policies rests in our lack of adherence to God's prophetic call that we care for the orphan, widow, and refugee among us. Whenever the people of God begin to move away from worshiping God in both word and deed, it creates injustice in our culture.

However, the hope of the good news of Jesus Christ is that we are not left on our own. Our hearts of stone are replaced by hearts of flesh that can (miracles of miracles!) create unity among the people of God. We Christians believe that ultimately, this heart of flesh is found in the one Israelite whose heart was never stony, Jesus Christ (Jenson, 99).

1. Are there aspects of these passages that make you squeamish? Can you see any good news poking through the discomfort?

_____

_____

_____

_____

_____

2. When you imagine the "glory of God," what images come to mind? Are they similar to or different from Ezekiel's?

_____

_____

_____

_____

_____

3. What are some ways that churches can keep God as the center of their worship?

_____

_____

_____

_____

_____

4. What aspects of Christian worship most connect you to God?

_____

_____

_____

_____

_____

5. The political leaders, Pelatiah and Benaiah, had grown narcissistic about their own abilities. How do we find the balance between being proud of our accomplishments and remaining humble?

_____

_____

_____

_____

_____

6. What are some injustices in your community that you feel are often ignored?

_____

_____

_____

_____

_____

7. God delivers a word of hope to the exiles in Babylon. Are there any people groups in our world today whom you think can relate to the experience of the exiles?

_____

_____

_____

_____

_____

8. *New Testament Connection:* Read again the portion of Jesus' prayer in John 17:20-24. How can you contribute to deeper unity among the people of God?

_____

_____

_____

_____

_____

9. Have you ever felt (or do you still feel) as if God has abandoned you?

_____

_____

_____

_____

_____

10. How do you reconcile the violent imagery that is sometimes used by the Old Testament prophets?

_____

_____

_____

_____

_____

5

Sour Grapes

Ezekiel 18:1-32

"Every generation imagines itself to be more intelligent than the one that went before it, and wiser than the one that comes after it."

—George Orwell, *Collected Essays* (4:51)

Whenever my Grandpa Simmons needed help with something, he would look at me and say, "Tyler, if you help me rake these leaves, I'll dance at your wedding in a pig trough." It was a strange saying that Grandpa likely picked up from working in the cotton fields of northeast Arkansas on his family farm. All cultures have specific idioms that reveal something about that culture and convey an idea figuratively. For example, in Japan, if you want someone to be brutally honest, you tell them "not to put clothes on your teeth." In Yiddish, if you want someone to leave you alone, you could tell them to "grow like an onion with your head in the ground." My favorite is the equivalent to "I'm not pulling your leg" in Russian: "I'm not hanging noodles on your ears."

Idioms are culturally specific sayings, and in Ezekiel 18 we find the prophet Ezekiel having to deal with a saying that was passed around the communities of exiles in Babylon. He confronts this idiom to remind people that God is ultimately about justice and that, even in exile, they have a responsibility to be God's chosen, set-apart people in the world.

"And" or "But" (18:1-4)

Our passage begins with the familiar formula we've seen multiple times before: the word of the Lord comes to Ezekiel. However, usually that phrase is followed by instructions to Ezekiel about how he is supposed to tell the people God's message. Instead, here in Ezekiel 18, God jumps straight into what God wants to say. Perhaps God so passionately wants to address this concern that God is dispensing with the normal formalities (Jenson, 144).

What God (through Ezekiel) wants to address is a statement that was on the lips of those in exile: "The parents have eaten sour grapes, and the children's teeth are set on edge." Evidently, this was a common saying during the Babylonian exile because the prophet Jeremiah also addressed its use (see Jer 31:29-30). But the idiom itself can be a difficult to translate, and its meaning changes depending on how we translate the conjunction. The word *vav* can be translated as either "and" or "but," and how we look at this proverb will determine how we view God's response.

If we choose to translate *vav* as "and," then the saying reads, "Parents eat sour grapes, and the children are the ones whose teeth are on edge," meaning it is inevitable that all children pay for the sins of their parents. This way of reading the idiom would lead us to think that the exilic community has bought into a kind of fatalism in which they simply accept their fate. They are saying to themselves, "It doesn't matter what we do or how we act because God is punishing us, and there is nothing we can do about it."

However, if we choose to translate *vav* as "but," then the meaning changes: "Parents eat sour groups, but it's the children whose teeth are on edge." This time the saying means, "Isn't God unfair? The parents are the ones who make the dumb decisions, and God makes their kids pay the price!" Rather than fatalism, this way of understanding the idiom is a kind of blame-shifting. The exiles are laying the blame for their current predicament at the feet of God's pettiness and also at the feet of their predecessors for all the mistakes they have made (C. Wright 2001, 182).

Either way of understanding the idiom is acceptable in the Hebrew, and either translation is addressed by God's response to the people. God wants the people to remove this phrase from their tongues because it does not accurately reflect their situation. Instead, God says that every human life matters to God. If the people are being fatalistic (*vav* = "and"), then God is saying, "You are not simply a cog in a machine of punishment; you are my beloved people." If the people are blame-shifting (*vav* = "but"), then God is saying, "You cannot simply pass the buck for this punishment; you bear responsibility for your own actions and conduct."

Genogram Case Study (18:5-18)

Ezekiel demonstrates God's response by crafting a generational map of conduct. He lays before the people an example of a father, a son, and a grandson. If you've ever done any reading on family systems theory, you have likely heard the term "genogram" in which family behaviors and cycles are mapped out to see if patterns emerge that need addressing.

Ezekiel begins with the conduct of a man (the first generation) whose behavior is described as "lawful and right" (v. 5). In Hebrew, this man would be considered a *zaddiq*, a "righteous man." In Israelite theology, a person whose life is defined by righteousness is one who has a deep concern for a neighborly ethic, and we can clearly see that in the qualities of this man. Ezekiel lists three areas where the man's righteousness is on full display: *faith*, *sexuality*, and *economics*:

- The man demonstrates his righteousness through *faith* in his avoidance of idols (v. 6a). He refuses to bow down to idols placed in the mountain camps of surrounding peoples, and he recognizes the idolatry that has infiltrated the temple community (see Session 3, "Idol Hands").
- The man demonstrates his righteousness through his *sexuality* (v. 6b). The man maintains his marriage vows and adheres to the Levitical standards of refraining from sexual intercourse during a woman's menstrual period (which was likely a reminder to men that women are not sexual objects to be used by men; women have their own autonomy).

This is a controversial point to make in our current cultural climate in which any infringement on sexual expression is seen as oppressive. Certainly, the church has not always conducted itself with gentleness and love in addressing issues of sexuality. However, the point remains that even something as seemingly private as our sex lives is under the sovereignty of our Creator God. As Christopher Wright says in his book *Old Testament Ethics*, "Ezekiel would have had no patience with the curious modern idea that people's private sexual life and infidelities have no bearing on their public integrity or trustworthiness" (C. Wright 2004, 374).

- The man demonstrates his righteousness through *economics* (vv. 7-8). The ways the righteous man handles his money receive the longest comment from Ezekiel. As an employer, the man pays a fair and living wage, he gives charitably to the poor in his community, and he does not seek to profit through interest on loans he has given to his neighbors.

Some of us may be squirming a bit at this point. Many of us are uncomfortable when we feel that preachers start messing with our wallets. Yet Ezekiel maintains that righteousness must be defined by a neighborly economy that involves practices of equity and justice (Brueggemann 2016, 152–53).

While this man's life may be defined by righteousness, his son (the second generation) has chosen a different path and is a person of idolatry, toxic sexuality, and oppressive economic practices (vv. 10-13). Ezekiel declares that the righteousness of this man's father does not save him from just punishment, but God will hold him responsible for his own conduct. However, the original man's grandson (the third generation) lives a life defined by righteousness in the same vein as his grandfather (vv. 14-18).

The Righteous and the Wicked (18:19-24)

After hearing about these three generations, the people say to Ezekiel, "Why shouldn't the son suffer for the iniquity of the father?" They respond with surprise and say, "Wait a minute. Why does the grandson not suffer punishment because of his father's unrighteousness? After all, that's what is happening to us! Haven't you heard the saying about sour grapes?" (C. Wright 2001, 191). The exiles feel this way because they have cast themselves in the role of the third generation; they see themselves as righteous and the generation before them as wicked. They assume they were sent into exile as punishment for their parents' sins. But Ezekiel tells them that they are the second generation! They are in exile because of their own behavior, and they cannot lay the blame elsewhere. Therefore, says God, they cannot resort to blame-shifting.

However, God also does not allow for fatalism. For God reminds the exiles that while they are held responsible for their wickedness, they may always seek the path of repentance and righteousness (vv. 21-24). One commentator calls this "the Gospel according to Ezekiel," and I think that's an apt description. Ezekiel reminds the people that God is not a vindictive, cruel tyrant who takes pleasure in death. Instead, God seeks a relationship with all people that is defined by covenantal love and righteous, neighborly behavior.

Whose Ways Are Truly Unfair? (18:25-29)

The people still don't feel that the ways of God add up. They cry out, "But that's unfair!" Evidently, the notion that children are to be punished for their parents' behavior was so innately ingrained in their psyches that any alternative was not only unfathomable but even offensive. After all, the scandal of the gospel for many people is not how exclusive grace can be but who is included in this grace (even them!).

God turns the question around on them and says, "You think my ways are unfair? Have you had a look at yourselves?" Returning again to the tangible acts of righteousness, God accuses the people of having no moral insight into their own wickedness. Just like the exiles, we in the twenty-first-century Western world take great pride in how progressive and justice-oriented our society can be. We look down our noses at past generations or at cultures different from ours and pat ourselves on the back for how enlightened we are. While we have certainly made many moral achievements in our day and time, we cannot allow those accomplishments to blind us to the issues of wishy-washy faith, of toxic sexuality, and of oppressive and unjust economic practices that still exist. When we lament over the injustice in the world, here in Ezekiel 18 God wants us to take a good, long look in the mirror before we start trying to point fingers elsewhere.

Repent and Turn (18:30-32)

The chapter ends with good news that is both life-giving and challenging. It is life-giving because we are not set on a predetermined, fatalistic path with no options for change. Instead, God provides the exiles (and us) with a path for returning to a covenantal relationship with God. However, this good news is challenge because it is not, to use Dietrich Bonhoeffer's phrase, "cheap grace." It requires a change of heart and a change of behavior. Otherwise, this message produces no actual change in the people. As Bonhoeffer writes in *The Cost of Discipleship*,

> Cheap grace is the preaching of forgiveness without requiring repentance, baptism without church discipline, Communion without confession, absolution without personal confession. Cheap grace is grace without discipleship, grace without the cross, grace without Jesus Christ, living and incarnate. (44)

It requires a change of heart and a change of behavior.

Conclusion

Repentance in the Bible is never merely a matter of words, and it is not simply a spiritual or emotional attitude. It is always about reconciliation and putting things right even (and especially) when it costs us something. It is uncomfortable to talk about religion, sexuality, and economics. In our pluralistic world, we don't care for language teeming with exclusivity toward one faith, but God will not have the "all-paths-lead-to-the-same-place" syncretism that defines our modern world. In a sexually liberated world, we balk at any restrictions on our sexual expression, but God requires that we never treat other people as objects and that commitment define our sexual lives. In our capitalistic world, we have no interest in faith affecting our wallets, but God will not allow us to compartmentalize our lives apart from the gospel. We must help build a world that shows we are a people with a new heart and a new spirit, so we must take a hard look at the unjust and unrighteous practices of our own society when it comes to religion, sexuality, and economics.

1. What are idioms or strange sayings that you grew up hearing?

_____

_____

_____

_____

_____

2. Are you someone who is prone to fatalism, thinking that nothing you do really matters? If so, what tends to help bring you out of that kind of thinking?

_____

_____

_____

_____

_____

3. Do you think people are punished for the behaviors of past generations?

_____
_____
_____
_____
_____

4. How do you wrestle with respecting others' religious beliefs and also holding to your own beliefs with conviction?

_____
_____
_____
_____
_____

5. Why do so many people avoid the topic of sexuality when it comes to faith?

_____
_____
_____
_____
_____

6. Can you think of unjust economic practices that exist in your own community? What can you do to help makes things right?

_____
_____
_____
_____
_____

7. Is there a difference between fairness and justice?

_____
_____
_____
_____
_____

8. *New Testament Connection:* Read Jesus' parable of the workers in the vineyard from Matthew 20:1-16. How do you connect Ezekiel 18 with the message of this story told by Jesus?

_____

_____

_____

_____

_____

9. What are ways that our society continues to be "unfair" in practice?

_____

_____

_____

_____

_____

10. What do you think of when you hear the word "repent," and does that perception need to change?

_____

_____

_____

_____

_____

Pride Cometh before the Fall
Ezekiel 28:1-19

First pride, then the crash —
the bigger the ego, the harder the fall.
                                        —Proverbs 16:18, *The Message*

Françoise Gilot first met Pablo Picasso in 1943. At the time, she was twenty-one, and the world-renowned artist was forty years her senior. They began a relationship with one another. She was an aspiring artist and found proximity to Picasso's creative genius to be intoxicating. However, the relationship was also abusive. In her memoir, *Life with Picasso*, Gilot describes how Picasso would say things to her such as "Women are machines for suffering" and "For me there are only two kinds of women: goddesses and doormats." He physically abused Gilot and even put out a cigarette on her face. In the memoir, Gilot describes how she once heard Picasso whispering to somebody over and over, "I am God. I am God. I am God" (Gilot and Lake). What fueled Picasso's abuse? What led to this level of narcissism? Many factors could be to blame, but it seems that a good starting place is to acknowledge that Picasso had a heightened view of himself and a lowered view of God.

The scene from Ezekiel 28 deals with those kinds of issues: how we view ourselves and how we view God. The passage takes place in a long series of oracles against nations that surrounded ancient Israel such as Moab, Philistia, Egypt, and Tyre (Ezek 25–32). In these diatribes, God judges the nations for their lack of response to (or even acknowledgment of their complicity in) the Babylonian exile of God's people. Chapter 28 deals specifically with the king of Tyre and what happens when a nation loses perspective on whom God has called them to be.

Just Who Do You Think You Are? (28:1-10)

Ezekiel now begins to preach directly to the prince of Tyre, the leader of a seafaring people to the north of Israel. This sermon does not begin with a cute story or even some of Ezekiel's famous street theatrics. Instead, Ezekiel immediately launches into using the prince's own words against him. The prince has evidently been proclaiming, "I am a god." As evidence of his divine status, the prince boasts about his home being in "the heart of the seas" (v. 2). In ancient Sumerian texts, there are stories of gods who built their home in the seas, on mountains that rose from the waters. Some kings in the ancient Near East would build their palaces near the coast in an effort to imitate the gods (Walton and Keener, 1382). Perhaps the location of his home has created a sense of entitlement in the heart of the prince of Tyre.

But it's not just a beach house that causes the prince's hubris. He also has both wisdom and wealth. Ezekiel compares the prince to the great Hebrew hero Daniel, who demonstrated his wisdom and resolve in the court of the empire. Ezekiel is not disputing that the prince of Tyre indeed possesses wisdom. However, there are vast differences between the prince of Tyre and Daniel. Whereas Daniel rose in the ranks of the royal court and was wise enough to be content with his position, the prince of Tyre was greedy for more and more (Block 1998, 97). Ezekiel accuses the prince of abusing his God-given wisdom in the pursuit of exorbitant wealth.

Because of the prince's pride in his wisdom and wealth, and because he has claimed to be among the pantheon of gods, Ezekiel declares to this royal ruler that he will be overthrown by other nations. With no small hint of snark, in verse 7 Ezekiel uses some of the same language for the prince of Tyre that is used for how idols are treated after a conquest. Ezekiel is saying, "You want to call yourself a god? Fine. Then you will receive the treatment of all the other false gods" (Odell, 361). Ezekiel dares to declare to the prince of Tyre, "You shall die the death of the uncircumcised" (v. 10). Circumcision was the symbol of God's beloved, set-apart people in the world. Because of the prince of Tyre's hubris and pride, God is refusing to acknowledge any recognition of who he is.

The Protestant reformer Martin Luther said that sin is *homo incurvatus in se*, a human being turned in on itself. Nearly all the sin in our lives goes back to pride: we think we can do whatever we want, we think we know how best to order the world, we think we have all the answers, etc. We may not use these words exactly, but pride tricks us into thinking we are gods. That is one of the reasons we have days on the church calendar that remind us of our humanity and our mortality. On Ash Wednesday, we receive a cross on our foreheads and are told, "Remember that you are dust, and to dust you shall return." It is difficult to be prideful about our wisdom or wealth when we are reminded that our lives are gifts from God.

Another day on the church calendar when we face our own mortality is All Saints' Day, which is usually commemorated on the first Sunday in November. In my church (as in many traditions), we read the names of the members of our congregation who have passed over the previous year. Each year I think about them and am grateful for the time I shared with them. But I am also struck each year with the sober reminder that one day my name will be on that list, spoken aloud as a chime is rung in my memory. The prince of Tyre had lost sight of what it means to be human, to embrace the limits of our nature and to express gratitude to God, the giver of life itself.

On All Saints' Day in 2014, Pope Francis preached a homily on the need for humanity never to play the part of God because, when we do, destruction always follows:

> Man takes control of everything, he believes he is God, he believes he is king. And wars, the wars that continue, they do not exactly help to sow the seed of life but to destroy. It is an industry of destruction. It is also a system, also of life, that when things cannot be fixed they are discarded: we discard children, we discard the old, we discard unemployed youth. This devastation has created the culture of waste. We discard people. (Vatican)

The Fall of a Nation (28:11-19)

After his sermon addressing the prince of Tyre, Ezekiel raises up a lamentation for the "king of Tyre." It is strange for Ezekiel to suddenly switch titles. Some scholars believe this is because verses 11-19 are addressed not just to the prince of Tyre but also to the nation itself. It was not uncommon for addresses to the "king" of a people to be intended for the entire country.

Ezekiel begins this portion with lofty language that takes us back to the creation stories in Genesis 1–3. The garden of Eden is a metaphor for the great height from which Tyre has fallen (C. Wright 2001, 244). Eden is not referenced much outside of Genesis, but when it is, it symbolizes how God originally dreamed the world would work (see Isa 51:3; Joel 2:3). The kingdom of

Tyre is described as having originally helped to fulfill God's dream. Ezekiel even uses the colorful language of jewelry that we have sometimes seen him employ for God's presence. Metaphorically, precious gems once adorned the kingdom of Tyre. Daniel Block points out that many of the gems listed in verse 13 are the same stones worn by the high priest in the temple (Block 1998, 106–10). Why would a foreign nation wear the precious jewels of the high priest? This may go back to the image of the garden of Eden. Adam, the original man, was meant to be God's representative in the world, but he failed. The high priest, when performing his ministerial duties, served as a symbol of God's representative to the people. But the mission of God's people in the world was not that only Adam or the high priest would represent God's nature and character; it was that a set-apart, holy people would show who God is. The fact that even Tyre is included among the people who were set apart shows the ever-expanding inclusivity of God's sovereignty and grace. An alternative reason for the king of Tyre wearing the jewels of the high priest is that Ezekiel is slipping in a criticism of both the traders and the religious leaders of Israel. He may even be indicting Israel's high priest through this veiled portrait of the king of Tyre. So, while Ezekiel is railing against the violent and unjust practices of Tyre, he is simultaneously accusing Israel's merchants and priests of greed and economic oppression (Creach, 169–71).

However we may solve the mystery of why Tyre is included here, one thing is sure: something happened and changed the people's status. The word "Tyre" means "stone," and in verse 15 Ezekiel says that "iniquity was found in you." The Hebrew word he uses for "iniquity" can also be translated "cracks" (Odell, 363). The nation who considered itself to be on rock-solid footing is now watching things crumble around it. The reason for Tyre's changed status is clearly laid out: "In the abundance of your trade you were filled with violence, and you sinned" (v. 16). The success of Tyre's economy brought with it a change in national character. It seems that the country cared more about the bottom line than about whether its financial systems allowed the people to commit acts of violence for the sake of the profit. Rather than gratitude to God for the gifts it had received, the nation of Tyre seems to have used its vast wealth to further fill its coffers. God had enough. As Block writes, "The exploitation of a divinely bestowed privilege to satisfy one's personal greed and ambition calls for divine intervention" (Block 1998, 120).

Some of the language used for the king of Tyre in verses 11-19 has led interpreters to believe that this passage is about an even more cosmic figure. Is this passage about Satan? The language certainly fits some of the story many of us have been told about the origins of Satan. And Ezekiel 28:11-19 (together with Isaiah 14:3-23) is seen as Old Testament evidence of Satan's origins. Many people grow up learning that Lucifer was the most beautiful of all the angels ("Your heart was proud because of your beauty," v. 17a) and rebelled against God. Lucifer and his armies of angels were cast down to hell because of their betrayal ("I cast you to the ground," v. 17b).

We don't have space to go into all the history of interpretation around the character of Satan in Christianity (see De La Torre and Hernandez). But the commonly believed story about the origin of Satan comes more from John Milton's *Paradise Lost* than it does from the Bible. The reformer John Calvin never wrote a commentary on Ezekiel, but he did write one on Isaiah. In Isaiah 14, the prophet speaks about the fall of the king of Babylon in terms similar to Ezekiel's passage about Tyre. Calvin wrote this about the interpretation that these passages might refer to the devil: "The context plainly shows that these statements must be understood in reference to the king of the Babylonians. But when passages of Scripture are taken up at random, and no attention is paid to the context, we need not wonder that mistakes of this kind frequently arise" (in Block 1998, 119).

Rather than being about Satan, Ezekiel 28:11-19 is a lamentation about what happens when nations are boastful about their resources and unjust in their economics. Like Adam in the garden of Eden or the high priest in the temple, those with power have a special calling to represent God in the world. But when they allow their power to corrupt them, and they fail to use their resources to care for the poor and the marginalized in their midst, they no longer serve as God's ambassadors for reconciliation. Fire may burn within them because of their pride, but God will allow that fire to consume them. They have forgotten that they are dust, and to dust they shall return.

Conclusion

Ezekiel 28 is about the pitfalls of pride, both for individuals and for nations. Our world seems to be seeing an increase in authoritarian leaders who prop themselves up as the only ones capable of bringing peace to our world. Sadly, many people are drawn to political leaders who thrive on arrogance and boasting. As lamentable as that may be, we cannot lay the blame for the society's ills solely at the feet of a handful of psychologically unhealthy leaders. The sin of pride runs through every human heart, and we each risk falling into the trap of the prince of Tyre, taking pride in our resources and seeing ourselves as "self-made." We need to place our hope outside of what we own or what we have achieved and instead rely on the mercy, grace, and holiness of God, the one in whom we live and move and have our being (Acts 17:28).

1. What does it look like in our world when people claim to be like God?

_____

_____

_____

_____

_____

2. Our world has been through a great deal of reckoning about how people with power treat others. How do you reconcile the artistic mastery of someone like Picasso with his abysmal treatment of women?

_____

_____

_____

_____

_____

3. The ancient world sometimes connected wisdom and wealth. Does our world today still do that, or do we view the two concepts differently?

_____

_____

_____

_____

_____

4. What do you make of Martin Luther's definition of sin as *homo incurvatus in se* ("a human turned in on itself")?

_____

_____

_____

_____

_____

5. Are there specific moments in worship that remind you how we are to view God and how we are to view ourselves?

_____

_____

_____

_____

_____

6. *New Testament Connection:* Read Acts 12:19-23. What connections can you find between the prince of Tyre and King Herod?

_____

_____

_____

_____

_____

7. What does it mean to be God's set-apart people in the world?

_____

_____

_____

_____

_____

8. Why does a nation's economic practices reveal the heart of who its people are?

_____

_____

_____

_____

_____

9. *New Testament Connection:* Read Revelation 17–18. In this passage from Revelation, John depicts the fall of the Roman Empire as "the Fall of Babylon." As you read these passages, can you name the reasons given for the empire's downfall?

_____

_____

_____

_____

_____

10. What is so dangerous about any government claiming to have divine status?

_____

_____

_____

_____

_____

The True Shepherd

Ezekiel 34:1-31

"Leadership is about integrity, honesty and accountability.
All components of trust."

—Simon Sinek, *Leaders Eat Last* (150)

I am an avid podcast listener. Recently, alongside thousands of others, I've been devouring the episodes of Christianity Today's podcast called *The Rise and Fall of Mars Hill*. It's the story of a mega-church in Seattle called Mars Hill and the charismatic and brash pastor who founded the church, Mark Driscoll. The podcast details how the culture of Mars Hill church became toxic and justifiably lays the blame on the shoulders of the leaders. It's a foreboding story of the devastating consequences of toxic leadership.

Toxic and abusive leadership is the problem Ezekiel tackles in chapter 34. However, as we come to this text, we are entering into a land of hopefulness in the book of Ezekiel. Chapters 1–24 are mostly diatribes against the people of Israel, and chapters 25–32 are judgment oracles against foreign nations. Chapter 33 serves as a hinge chapter in which themes about Ezekiel's prophetic vocation are repeated. Moving into chapters 34–39 is like waking up to a cool autumn morning after a blistering summer. The theme of these chapters is restoration. Although Ezekiel deals with some difficult topics in chapter 34, the result is one in which God will bring wholeness and healing. God will bring healing to the people in holistic ways: spiritually, socially, relationally, and politically. Try as we might in our culture, we cannot compartmentalize those facets of society from one another. Only a truly gracious shepherd can provide everything the sheep need.

Bad Shepherds (34:1-10)

In the ancient world, it was common to compare political and societal leaders to shepherds. Shepherds were appointed caretakers of an owner's flock; likewise, leaders are divinely appointed caretakers of a people. The sheep (the people) had an owner (the gods), and the shepherd (the king) was charged with providing for and protecting the owner's property. Therefore, if something untoward happened to the sheep, the shepherd was liable since he had failed in his responsibilities. That is the charge that Ezekiel makes against the shepherds of Israel in this passage. There are several possibilities as to what specific leaders Ezekiel has in mind. It could be that he is speaking of the leaders of the remnant in Jerusalem who have already been the subject of much prophetic ire. However, he could also be making a sweeping statement about the kings of Judah, who for a century (almost without exception) failed to be godly leaders and instead sought to expand their own wealth and prestige (C. Wright 2001, 274). Regardless of whether he is indicting leaders of the past or the present, Ezekiel's charge remains the same: these shepherds have failed to care for God's sheep.

In verse 3, Ezekiel begins by saying that they have availed themselves of the three by-products most common from sheep: the fat (which referred to the milk curds), the wool, and the mutton. There was nothing inherently wrong with a shepherd using these resources from a sheep. But their permission to glean from the sheep was predicated on the belief that they would, in return, provide adequate protection for the sheep. Otherwise, they were simply exploiting a resource that did not belong to them. In verse 4, that is exactly what Ezekiel accuses them of doing. While they have been eating curds, selling wool, and chewing the meat, they have also failed to strengthen the weak, heal the sick, care for the injured, or seek out the lost and wandering lambs (Walton and Keener, 1395).

Simon Sinek, a well-known thinker in the area of leadership, wrote *Leaders Eat Last*; the title comes from Sinek's experience of watching marines eat in a mess hall. The higher the rank of the marine, the farther they went toward the back of the line to get their food. This small act of self-sacrifice paid enormous dividends in the unity and trust built among the marines. Sinek says,

> If our leaders are to enjoy the trappings of their position in the hierarchy, then we expect them to offer us protection. The problem is, for many of the overpaid leaders, we know that they

took the money and perks and didn't offer protection to their people. In some cases, they even sacrificed their people to protect or boost their own interests. This is what so viscerally offends us. We only accuse them of greed and excess when we feel they have violated the very definition of what it means to be a leader. (65)

The list of responsibilities Ezekiel says the leaders have failed to live up to goes slightly beyond normal shepherding duties. Instead, Ezekiel begins to dive into kingship territory. When he speaks of the weak and vulnerable, he is referring to the marginalized in society who often rely on the king's justice for survival. The law of Israel has countless commands for the people (and specifically for leadership) that they are to provide care for the widows, orphans, and refugees among them (see Exod 22:21-24; Jas 1:27). In a speech in 1977, former vice president Hubert Humphrey said it well: "The moral test of government is how that government treats those who are in the dawn of life, the children; those who are in the twilight of life, the elderly; those who are in the shadows of life, the sick, the needy, and the handicapped" (quoted in Knight).

God's patience has run out on the shepherds failing to protect and care for the sheep. God has seen that the people are leaderless and wandering around with no guidance. Therefore, God says, "No longer shall the shepherds feed themselves. I will rescue my sheep from their mouths, so that they may not be food for them" (v. 10). God has decided, "If you want to do something right, you have to do it yourself."

The True Shepherd (34:11-22)

God is the true shepherd of the people. This is a theme throughout the Old Testament narratives. In 1 Samuel 8, the people corner the judge Samuel and demand that they be given a king so that they can be like the neighboring nations. Both God and Samuel raise a protest and say, "But don't you see? You were never meant to be like the other nations. They put their faith in a human king, but you follow the Creator of the universe!" However, the people continue to demand a king, and God condescends to their pleas. But here in Ezekiel 34, we see that the story has come full circle back to the original intent of God's people. They are to be set apart from the rest of the world and not follow the "shepherds" who will invariably disappoint and abuse them. Instead, God is their shepherd and king.

In this passage, God shepherds the people in three ways:

• *Gathering* (vv. 11-13a)—Shepherds would often gather their flocks together to both count the sheep and protect from harm. Here, God is bringing together the scattered sheep of Israel so that they may be brought back into the fold of God's people. Surely, to Ezekiel's audience in exile who continue to feel separated from God in the land of Babylon, this is truly good news to their souls.

• *Feeding* (vv. 13b-16)—One of the shepherd's primary tasks was to guide the sheep toward land that was rich in nutrients and water. Psalm 23, one of the most beloved portions of Scripture, imagines God as a shepherd who provides what we need: "The LORD is my shepherd, I shall not want. He makes me lie down in green pastures; he leads me beside still waters; he restores my soul" (Ps 23:1-3a).

• *Justice* (vv. 17-22)—The role of a shepherd was not all tranquil pictures of serenity. They had to maintain order and protect the sheep, even from other sheep. God seems to be accusing some of the sheep of trampling the ground and soiling the water. They are called "fat sheep" because they have been willing to destroy the resources meant for others just so they can feed their greed. Ezekiel is calling out "bullies" among the people who seek to profit from the crisis, who seek only their self-interests, and who have abandoned a neighborly ethic. An ecological concern is at play here as well. The "fat sheep" are consuming the resources and stripping the land of its usefulness. God, the good shepherd, must now step in and administer justice by determining who is acting selfishly and who is truly in need.

Christians read stories in the Gospels where Jesus is the ultimate fulfillment of the image of a truly good shepherd. In the Gospel of John, Jesus draws upon this image when he dares to declare, "I am the good shepherd. The good shepherd lays down his life for the sheep" (John 10:11). Jesus draws on this image from Ezekiel to picture himself as the good shepherd for all people who gathers a scattered flock (John 10:16) and who provides green pasture for the soul (John 10:8). The Gospel of Matthew contains the haunting parable of a final, global judgment in which "All the nations will be gathered before him [the Son of Man], and he will separate people one from another as a shepherd separates the sheep from the goats" (Matt 25:32). In Jesus' parable, the difference between the sheep and the goats is that the true sheep of God's flock have retained their neighborly ethic by feeding the hungry, giving drink to the thirsty, welcoming the stranger, clothing the naked, caring for the sick, and visiting the prisoner. The goats, on the other hand, have neglected to care for the least among them.

A Restored Prince (34:23-24)

A small portion of this hopeful oracle is a prayer for the restoration of the monarchy as it should function. The exiles still have a glimmer of hope for continuing the dynasty of David, a 400-year-old kingly family with good intentions (and mixed results). For the people of Israel in exile, David symbolized what it would look like for them to be fully restored as God's people. However, an interesting detail in these two verses is worth pondering. As much hope as Ezekiel places in a Davidic monarch, the word "king" is avoided here. Since God has already announced that God will be the people's true shepherd-king, Ezekiel seems to downplay the role of a human ruler (C. Wright 2001, 280). Instead of a "king," this new monarch will be a "prince" who will act as an ambassador of the true king.

A Covenant of Peace (34:25-31)

Once the proper leadership is in place with God as king-shepherd and a Davidic ruler as prince over the people, Ezekiel tells us that God will reestablish a covenant with God's people and that this covenant will be made of "peace" (Heb., *shalom*). Much has been written about the holistic meaning of *shalom* that goes far beyond merely the cessation of conflict (for example, see Brueggemann 1982). *Shalom* in the Bible is about a sense of wholeness, harmony, and safety that pervades the entire created order. The benefits of this covenant of peace are a reversal of the curses listed for breaking God's covenant in Leviticus 26 (Darr, 317–18). For an exiled people who have already expressed belief in the inevitability of their cursed status, seeing these curses reversed would bring inexpressible hope. There are three main blessings from this covenant of peace:

• *Safety from wild animals* (vv. 25, 27b-28)—Whereas Leviticus 26:22 promises that God will "let loose wild animals against you," verse 25 here promises that the wild animals' violent nature will be reversed. And in verses 27b-28, Ezekiel makes it clear that these wild animals are metaphors for the surrounding nations that have

The True Shepherd

threatened to enslave and endanger God's people. The covenant of shalom will bring diplomatic peace to all people.

• *God's people will be a blessing* (v. 26)—Notice that verse 26 does not say, "I will give them blessings," but instead says, "I will make them and the region around my hill a blessing." This harks back to the covenant in Genesis 12:1-3 in which God blesses Abram not so that he may become wealthier or gain more prestige but so that he and his family might *be* a blessing to the rest of the world. God's people always reflect back to the world what God has given to us. "We love because God first loved us" (1 John 4:19). This new covenant of *shalom* will involve vocational peace to God's people.

• *Food security* (vv. 27a, 29)—In this covenant of peace made by God, the fertility of the land will be so great that the people will never again experience famine. This is another reversal of a curse found in Leviticus: "You shall sow your seed in vain" (Lev 26:16). Here in Ezekiel, there is more than enough fruit and vegetation to feed the people. Given that starvation and food security are at the root of so many international conflicts in human history, this abundance of provisions would lead to less battling among nations.

The closing verses of Ezekiel 34 return to the larger point of this entire chapter: given the failure of the current leaders, God will instead step in as shepherd of the people. However, we make a mistake if we think this means our job is to passively wait for God to act. Instead, we are called to be participants in the establishing of the covenant of peace. While God is the ultimate source of salvation, we must still work toward *shalom* in our own world.

The prophets in the Bible speak numerous times about a vision of *shalom* that will fundamentally alter all of creation. One of the most famous passages that shares much with Ezekiel 34 is Isaiah 11:1-9, in which "the wolf shall live with the lamb" (v. 6). The Quaker preacher and painter Edward Hicks painted nearly thirty versions of this passage between 1820 and 1849. One of the most famous versions depicts the animals in the passage lying peacefully with one another in the foreground. But in the background, early American settlers are entering into a peaceful relationship with Native Americans. Given the context of the nineteenth century and the failure of the United States government to serve as a beacon of peace, Hicks's painting was a radical depiction of what might be possible. And that is what prophets do: they dare to imagine what it might look like if God's people both dreamed of and worked toward a more peaceful world for all people.

Conclusion

The modern world seems to suffer from a leadership crisis. For decades, social psychologists have told us that the level of trust in human leaders such as politicians, journalists, and pastors is at an all-time low. This lack of trust easily calcifies into a kind of cynicism. Many people are deconstructing their faith—or separating from it altogether—as the leaders they formally followed without question turn out to be less than honorable. Ultimately, Ezekiel 34 is a reflection on the failure of human leadership. In a world that is currently so divided and hostile, many people have placed themselves in echo chambers or ideological camps where they invest their souls in their chosen leaders. Right or wrong, they will follow that leader no matter what. The Bible has a word for such behavior: idolatry. Idolatry is an infection of both the political right and the political left. The people of God are to reject any leader who seeks to claim our ultimate allegiance. Instead, we are to remember that the earliest Christian confession of faith was written in opposition to a common Roman phrase. Whereas the way of the world is to declare "Caesar is Lord," we are the people who confess with our lips and lives that "Jesus is Lord."

1. When have you seen a leader fail? How did it happen and what was the result?

_____

_____

_____

_____

_____

2. What are the qualities of a good leader?

_____

_____

_____

_____

_____

The True Shepherd

3. According to Scripture, what responsibilities does a society have to marginalized and vulnerable people?

_____

_____

_____

_____

_____

4. The last Sunday of the Christian calendar is Christ the King Sunday. What do you think it means to live as if Jesus Christ is our King without resorting to a kind of nationalism?

_____

_____

_____

_____

_____

5. What environmental responsibilities do we have to our neighbors?

_____

_____

_____

_____

_____

6. *New Testament Connection:* Read John 10:1-18. How can you see Jesus fulfilling this role of the ultimate good shepherd?

_____

_____

_____

_____

_____

7. What does *shalom* look like in our world?

_____
_____
_____
_____
_____

8. Read Psalm 23. What connections do you see between this beloved psalm and our passage from Ezekiel 34?

_____
_____
_____
_____
_____

9. *New Testament Connection:* Read Matthew 25:31-46. What are the connections between this parable from Matthew and the images from Ezekiel?

_____
_____
_____
_____
_____

10. How do we avoid placing our leaders on too high of a pedestal? Do we have any responsibility to them if/when they fail?

_____
_____
_____
_____
_____

The True Shepherd

A Heart Transplant

"The kingdom which Jesus came to bring on earth as in heaven must take root in, and be implemented through, the cleansed and softened hearts of his followers."
—N. T. Wright, *After You Believe* (123)

In C. S. Lewis's novel *The Lion, the Witch, and the Wardrobe*, the newly resurrected Lion (together with Susan and Lucy) invades the White Witch's castle. The Witch's fortress is full of stone statues that were formerly living beings who dared to stand up to her. Using her wand, she transforms them into stone. When Aslan and the girls enter the castle, they come upon another lion the Witch has turned to stone, frozen in a pouncing stance. Aslan walks up to the lion and breathes on it. Lucy says,

> "Oh, Susan! Look! Look at the lion."
> I expect you've seen someone put a lighted match to a bit of newspaper which is propped up in a grate against an unlit fire. And for a second nothing seems to have happened; and then you notice a tiny streak of flame creeping along the edge of the newspaper. It was like that now. For a second after Aslan had breathed upon him the stone lion looked just the same. Then a tiny streak of gold began to run along his white marble back—then it spread—then the colour seemed to lick all over him as the flame licks all over a bit of paper—then, while his hindquarters were still obviously stone, the lion shook his mane and all the heavy, stony folds rippled into living hair. Then he opened a great red mouth, warm and living, and gave a prodigious yawn. (154–55)

The healing breath of Aslan that transforms cold stone into warm flesh is reminiscent of Ezekiel 36. This passage is infused with images of hope, yet that hope arises from difficult and problematic texts. (Would we expect anything less from Ezekiel?) What emerges from the struggle here is a picture of spiritual formation that is worth a lifetime of reflection.

A Land Defiled (36:16-21)

Ezekiel believes that before there can be hope, there must be holiness (Brueggemann 1986, 71). Before there can be restoration of relationship, there must be acknowledgment of what led to the rift in the first place. God begins in this passage by speaking to Ezekiel as one speaks to a friend (Block 1998, 344). God's heart seems to be hurting over the division within the three-fold relationship between God, God's people, and the land. Namely, the people of God have defiled the land.

As a metaphor for the people's actions, Ezekiel uses an awkward image that should make us uncomfortable. He compares the people's actions to the ritually unclean nature of a woman during her menstrual cycle as laid out in the Levitical law (see Lev 15:1-33). While many male biblical commentators try to soften this image by trying to explain how Ezekiel's use of it is appropriate, such efforts do not amount to much. It must be acknowledged that it is unsettling and distasteful for Ezekiel to equate the people's sinful behavior with the natural process of the female body necessary for procreation (Darr, 336). However, even through the use of this inappropriate metaphor for the unclean nature of the people, Ezekiel provides an image of hope. In the Levitical law, menstruation was a type of uncleanness that a purification ritual could eradicate. It was not a permanent state but a liminal state of uncleanness that could be rectified through ritual washing. If Israel could be cleansed, then holy community was possible as the people would be readmitted to the presence of God (Bowen, 222–23). First, their behavior had to be addressed.

The concern for Ezekiel is that the people's behavior has rendered the land itself unclean and sullied. The two behaviors that have led to this offense are the shedding of blood and idolatry (v. 18). The wanton violence of the people and their systems of injustice have led God to declare them unfit to be sanctified as God's people. Further, they have failed in their spiritual fidelity to God and have instead sought after idols. God is disgusted by their behavior, and the word used for "idols" translates as "pellets of dung" (Block 1998, 346–47). God's heart is broken because the people have "profaned my holy name" (v. 20). To profane God's name does not mean to actively curse or blaspheme. Instead, Ezekiel uses the word "profane" as the antonym of "sacred." The people have not allotted to God the holiness God deserves; instead, they have treated the Lord lightly (C. Wright 2001, 289). There is also a missional component to keeping God's name sacred. Ezekiel has a deep concern about what the profaned name of God would mean to other nations. If other nations look upon the state of the people of Israel and see them as both exiled and corrupt, how does that reflect on the God they claim to worship? Would any of those nations ever be willing to enter into covenantal loyalty with such a God? No. This concern for God's name is rooted in the suffering of God on behalf of all people (Fretheim, 132).

Because of the people's behavior, the land itself has been defiled. There is a direct connection between the behavior of humanity and care of the earth. This is not a mystery to us as we continue to feel greater effects of climate change in our day and age. Wendell Berry is a poet, storyteller and farmer in Kentucky who has written extensively about the relationship between people and the land. In his book *The Gift of Good Land*, he acknowledges that any human use of creation will have an effect, but there are ways to do so that honor and protect the land:

> To live, we must daily break the body and shed the blood of Creation. When we do this knowingly, lovingly, skillfully, reverently, it is a sacrament. When we do it ignorantly, greedily, clumsily, destructively, it is a desecration. In such desecration we condemn ourselves to spiritual and moral loneliness, and others to want. (Berry 1981, 281)

In Ezekiel 36, God is upset that the people have defiled the land through the spilling of blood and through idolatry. The destruction of human life is an affront to creation itself, and harming creation shows that productivity and consumption have replaced the Creator God as lords over our lives.

A New Heart and a New Spirit (36:22-32)

Repairing this broken relationship between God, the people, and the land requires a fundamental transformation that can only be accomplished through the grace of God. While the people will certainly change through this alteration, God makes it clear that this is not taking place because of their righteous character but because it brings more glory to God: "It is not for your sake, O house of Israel, that I am about to act, but for the sake of my holy name" (v. 22). This may at first strike modern readers as selfishness on God's part, but these sorts of comments must be placed within the theological context of God's glory and holiness. For a holy God to settle for less is destructive not merely to the reputation of the divine name but also to those for whom the holy God cares. Further, we should read verse 22 as an example of Hebrew "relative negation," a way of speaking that communicates priority of one thing over another. Thus, Ezekiel is not denying that God is restoring the relationship with the people for the sake of the people but is prioritizing the fact that a restored relationship ultimately brings further glory to God (C. Wright 2001, 291).

God will act to bring restoration in multiple ways. First, God begins by gathering the scattered people from wherever they may be (both those in Israel and those in exile) as a mother hen gathers her wandering chicks (v. 24). Then, since the land and the relationship have been defiled through uncleanliness, God ritually bathes the people. They are made acceptable to live again in God's presence through this act of washing (v. 25). For Christians, baptism serves as the ritual symbol of our own restored relationship to God: "Baptism, which this prefigured, now saves you—not as a removal of dirt from the body, but as an appeal to God for a good conscience, through the resurrection of Jesus Christ" (1 Pet 3:21).

We then come to one of the most beloved passages in all of Ezekiel: the inner, spiritual transformation within the people as an act of God's grace. "A new heart I will give you," God says, "and a new spirit I will put within you; and I will remove from your body the heart of stone and give you a heart of flesh. I will put my spirit within you, and make you follow the statutes and be careful to observe my ordinances" (vv. 26-27). In the ancient world, the heart (Heb., *lev*) was the locus of decision-making, not just of emotions. The cold and ossified heart of stone that is often indifferent to the suffering of the world is transformed into the beating heart of flesh that responds with warmth. And the spirit (Heb., *ruah*) was the inner disposition of an individual, the seat of their motivations and personality (C. Wright 2001, 296). God will infuse the people with God's own spirit, an act of re-creation that harks back to when God crafted the first man from the dust of the ground and "breathed into his nostrils the breath of life" (Gen 2:7).

Genuine Christian spiritual formation is about the transformation of our inner lives. This opportunity for formation is possible not because of how pious we may be or how righteous we may be; it is an act of sheer grace. This heart and spirit transplant that God performs on the people makes a life of obedience possible (Brueggemann 1986, 75). For those of us who seek to follow Jesus, we must also submit even our inner lives to regeneration by the power of the Holy Spirit. Peter Scazzero has a book called *Emotionally Healthy Spirituality* in which he argues, "It's impossible to be spiritually mature while remaining emotionally immature." He believes that many people have bought into a model of Christian discipleship that addresses only the surface-level issues in our lives, whereas the gospel is meant to permeate the deepest parts of who we are. When we explore our families of origin, journey through the dark nights of the soul, embrace the limits on our lives, live into the rhythms of spiritual practices like Sabbath-keeping, and establish a rule of life, we are changed from the inside out.

Because of the indwelling of this new heart and new spirit, a return to the land is now possible (v. 28). God and the people live in the land together, and God will make the land abundant and fruitful (vv. 29-30). Creation itself will be redeemed by the restoration of the people: "For the creation waits with eager longing for the revealing of the children of God" (Rom 8:19). Interestingly, when the people return to the land, their waywardness will come to mind, and they will feel a sense of shame (v. 31). Who among us has not looked back at moments in our lives or decisions we have made and not felt a sense of shame about long-past events? If we are wise, that conviction is the fuel of resolve to learn from our mistakes and to live life differently.

A Land Restored (36:33-36)

Because of God's gracious act of transforming the hearts and spirits of the people, *shalom* is brought back to the land itself. The other nations who once saw the devastation of the people of Israel as a stain on God's character now see a land that abundantly provides enough food for all the people. Cities in Israel that were once ghost towns are now bustling with energy and life. And fields that were once fallow and barren are now brimming with new crops. There is a peaceful relationship between God, the people, and the land. Everything is in such harmony that the nation of Israel is now compared to the garden of Eden (v. 35). The promise of such a vision completely reverses the corruption, the sense of abandonment, and the shame of the exiles. It is an eschatological hope that restoration is possible because of the grace of God (Middleton, 105–106).

The Flock of God (36:37-38)

Ezekiel 36 ends on a note that reminds us of the shepherd imagery from chapter 34. The people of God are like a flock of sheep and God is the good shepherd who provides for their needs. The specific way that God provides in this section is by giving them fruitful abundance. With the land restored and with food available for all, the stage is set for a population explosion! The people are compared to flocks of sheep, jamming the streets of Jerusalem as they did during the appointed festival times. We can imagine the emotional resonance this would have on Ezekiel. Having grown up in a priestly family and having anticipated serving as a priest himself, the idea of the sheep returning to fill the streets of his beloved city means a restoration of the temple, a restoration of his land, and a restoration of his faith. I like to imagine tears coming to his eyes as that immense hope took his breath away. And it was all possible because of the holiness and love of God.

Conclusion

One of the dominant narratives in our world today is that most of the answers to the questions we have in this life are found by a deeper exploration of our Self, some supposedly inner and purer version of ourselves that has been tainted by society's expectations. The culture says if we can just free our Self from those constraints, we will be who we truly are meant to be. There is something beautiful in that narrative, but I also think we run the risk of drawing water from empty well. Ezekiel 36 teaches us that spiritual formation is not about a further exploration of the self but about a further reliance on the grace of God. The New Testament letter to the Ephesians speaks of God at work in our lives and, echoing Ezekiel, says, "For by grace you have been saved through faith; and this is not your own doing; it is the gift of God" (Eph 2:8).

1. What do you think it means to profane the name of God?

_____
_____
_____
_____
_____

2. Are there images in this passage (or elsewhere in Ezekiel) that make you uncomfortable?

_____
_____
_____
_____
_____

3. What is the connection between sin and the desecration of the land?

_____
_____
_____
_____
_____

4. How can broken relationships be repaired?

_____
_____
_____
_____
_____

5. How does our world think of the "heart" differently from the way it was viewed in the ancient world? How does that change the way you understand this passage?

_____

_____

_____

_____

_____

6. *New Testament Connection:* Read Romans 8:18-25. What does creation specifically wait for, and how does this connect to Ezekiel 36?

_____

_____

_____

_____

_____

7. Consider Peter Scazzero's thought: "It's impossible to be spiritually mature while remaining emotionally immature." What do you make of that?

_____

_____

_____

_____

_____

8. How can God's people work for a more harmonious relationship between the Creator, the people, and the land?

_____

_____

_____

_____

9. *New Testament Connection:* Read Revelation 21:1-5. How do you see parallels between God's promises in Revelation and in Ezekiel 36:33-36?

_____

_____

_____

_____

_____

10. When you think of the word "restoration," what images come to mind?

_____

_____

_____

_____

_____

A Heart Transplant

Sticks and Bones
Ezekiel 37:1-28

"A dream is the bearer of a new possibility, the enlarged horizon, the great hope."
—Howard Thurman, *Disciplines of the Spirit* (45)

Jesmyn Ward's haunting novel *Sing, Unburied, Sing* is set in Mississippi and tells the story of teenage Jojo; his mother, Leonie; and the ghost of a boy named Richie. Like others in his family, Jojo has a supernatural ability to hear voices when others cannot. He hears the thoughts of animals on the family property and the laments of the dead. Richie was a prisoner in a local jail who had a violent and unjust death. His spirit haunts the family, who can hear the cries of the undead. "'There's so many,' Richie says. His voice is molasses slow. 'So many of us,' he says. 'Hitting. The wrong keys. Wandering against. The song'" (Ward, Kindle ed.).

Like Jojo, Ezekiel can hear the cries of the dead—perhaps not audibly, but the senses of loss and pain that accompany the experience of exile haunt him and his people like ghosts who cannot move on from this world. However, here in Ezekiel 37 we have two images that beautifully portray hope that lies beyond despair. The first image is the story of a desolate valley of bleached bones that are transformed into a spirit-filled people whose fleshy hearts now beat with life. The second image is a no-less-miraculous sign-act in which God will bring unifying healing to the divisions among the people.

Can These Bones Live? (37:1-14)

My seven-year-old son, Owen, loves skeletons. He loves to draw them in various dance moves, and he flips through library books to learn everything he can about bones. For Owen, skeletons are a thing to marvel and even laugh at. People today tend to laugh at skeletons as they comically move about in films or as we fight them in *Minecraft*. But in the ancient world, a skeleton would never have been seen as whimsical. Instead, if you were to encounter bare human bones in the world, you would interpret them as a sign of failure for this person's family, their community, and their god. An exposed skeleton meant that this person did not have a family who loved them enough to give them a proper burial, that their nation was not powerful enough to care for their dead, and that their god had abandoned them in their final moments.

In this passage, Ezekiel does not see one skeleton but an entire valley filled with dried, bleached-white bones exposed to the elements. Ezekiel has been taken to this valley through the power of "the hand of the LORD" (v. 1). This is the same phrase that begins Ezekiel's inaugural vision by the riverside (1:3) and the command from God for Ezekiel to perform street theater (3:22). This phrase also serves as an indication that Ezekiel is about to be used for a prophetic task on God's behalf. Given much of what God has asked of Ezekiel throughout this book, perhaps Ezekiel is bracing for year another demanding pronouncement from on high.

The hand of the Lord takes Ezekiel to a valley. The valley itself is not identified, and we will see throughout this vision that the imagery is meant to be metaphorical and symbolic. Rather than trying to identify the location of this valley on a map, it is more fruitful for us to compare it to the valleys in our souls. This is the valley of exile, the valley of despair, the valley of hopelessness that defines the experience of this broken people. And this valley is the antonym of the "high mountain" that had come to serve as a symbol of hope for the people (40:2; Duguid, 426). Once they are in the valley, God takes Ezekiel on a tour through the bones themselves, seemingly to verify that there is no life left here. As a priest, Ezekiel would have avoided contact with corpses, yet here God places him amid a legion of bones. This is another moment when we see that Ezekiel's idea of his vocation as a priest working in the temple has been transformed by his calling as a prophet.

God asks Ezekiel a question: "Mortal, can these bones live?" (v. 3). The obvious answer to this rhetorical question is "No," but Ezekiel seems to understand that this is not a normal question, and he passes the ball back to God: "O Lord GOD, you know" (v. 3). God then passes the ball straight back to Ezekiel and commands him, "Prophesy to these bones, and say to them: O dry bones, hear the word of the LORD" (v. 4). Perhaps we can imagine Ezekiel thinking to himself, "You know, God, you've asked me to do some crazy things before, but this really takes the cake. You want me to preach a sermon to a bunch of bones?" But that is exactly what God commands Ezekiel to do. That is what all preaching is: speaking on behalf of God even to situations that seem lifeless and without hope.

As with any good preacher, Ezekiel's sermon to the bones is to have a clear topic: "Thus says the Lord GOD to these bones: I will cause breath to enter you, and you shall live" (v. 5). The Hebrew word used here for breath is the word *ruah*, and it is found ten times in Ezekiel 37:1-14. It's the same word we encountered in 36:22-32 when God promised to bring a new spirit into the people. The word *ruah* is an enigmatic word in the Bible that can be understood as "breath," "wind," or "spirit," and we will see all three of those trans- lations in our passage. Ezekiel's sermon is about God's spirit (the New Testament will further develop this theological image into God's Holy Spirit) blowing across this desolate valley and somehow, mysteriously, bringing new life. Ezekiel even specifically mentions that the holy breath of God will cause the bones to move upright as veins, tendons, muscles, organs, and skin are all reconstituted into bodies. Having grown up in a priestly family and experienced in animal sacrifice, Ezekiel was probably familiar with anatomy (C. Wright 2001, 306). God is once again calling upon his former and intended life as a priest to confirm his new calling as a prophet.

Ezekiel does as he is told and preaches to the bones. He suddenly hears the spooky sound of dry bones rattling together. He watches as his words are brought to fruition and the various pieces of what make a human body are miraculously reunited. However, all is not complete. Because while the bodies look alive, they are not truly living, for "there was no breath in them" (v. 8). One needs only to consider our current culture's fascination with zombies to understand what this means. Movies and television depict hordes of human bodies aimlessly wandering, trying to feed a gnawing hunger that causes death and destruction to others. Inter- estingly, many of the zombie shows and films show these crowds of mindless bodies congregating in places of consumerism such as abandoned malls. Consumerism is a force that lulls us into thinking we are living meaningful lives, when really we are just zombies in the pursuit of serving an insatiable gnaw in our souls.

The valley of dry bones is now a valley full of bodies that are intact but without life. They lack breath and spirit (*ruah*). This harks back to the theological anthropology of the Old Testament: what makes a human? Back in Genesis 2, we encounter God crafting the first man (*adam*) out of the dust (*adamah*) of the ground (Gen 2:7a). Yet the molding and shaping of his body is only the first step in his creation. God then "breathed into his nostrils the breath (*ruah*) of life; and the man became a living being" (Gen 2:7b). In the Bible, to be fully human is to possess a body and to carry the divine breath within us. Interestingly, God turns to Ezekiel and commands him, "Prophesy to the breath (*ruah*), prophesy, mortal" (v. 9).

Why would God require Ezekiel to preach to the spirit of God? Couldn't God act without Ezekiel? Perhaps God chooses purposefully not to act alone. God's redemptive purposes for creation always involve God's people as ambassadors for reconciliation in the world (see 2 Cor 5:11-21). When Ezekiel preaches to the divine breath, he is commanded to speak to "the four winds (*ruah*)" (v. 9). In the ancient world, the phrase "the four winds" often referred to the four cardinal directions. It brings us back yet again to Ezekiel's inaugural vision of the wheels-within-wheels that can travel in any direction, symbolizing the mobility of God. Here, we have God's breath blowing into the valley from north, south, east, and west to deliver life-giving energy to the people (Block 1998, 377). It is also worth noting that perhaps the fact that the spirit comes from across the globe serves as a symbol for God's spirit being at work everywhere in the world, from all directions, and in places from which we have much to learn.

After preaching a twofold sermon to the bones and to the divine breath, Ezekiel watches as his words are brought to life. The valley of dry bones is transformed into a renewed and resurrected community. God says to Ezekiel, "Mortal, these bones are the whole house of Israel" (v. 11). It is easy to miss the beauty of what God is saying here. By saying that these are the "whole house of Israel," God is declaring that these resurrected bodies are not simply citizens of the southern kingdom of Judah who were victims of the Babylonian exile (597 BCE) but are also citizens of the northern kingdom of Israel who were victims of the Assyrian exile (740 BCE). God is declaring that God's people are now both resurrected and reunified (Block 1998, 379). This is altogether unexpected: God is not simply restoring the exiles to their former homes; God is restoring the entire nation to its former glory and is the only source of the possibility of new life. These dry bones are not simply walking on earth again; they are walking with the Lord again.

This is, without a doubt, the most well-known and loved passage from Ezekiel. Preachers tend to turn to it during Eastertide or Pentecost, and with good reason. It speaks about God's power to bring new life even into the valley of the shadow of death and offers us a picture of the resurrection of God's people. In our individual lives, we must be reminded that "you were dead through the trespasses and sin in which you once lived" (Eph 2:1-2). We too can metaphorically be the walking dead who wander through life living only to satisfy the hunger in our souls. "But God, who is rich in mercy, out of the great love with which he loved us even when we were dead through our trespasses, made us alive together with Christ—by grace you have been saved—and raised us up with him" (Eph 2:4-6). That is good news. Christians believe that the resurrection of Jesus Christ is the catalytic event for a new kind of creation characterized by hope over despair, salvation over sin, and life over death. As N. T. Wright says of Jesus' resurrection, "He is the firstfruits, the first to rise from the dead. But this isn't an isolated instance. The point of the firstfruits is that there will be many, many more" (2008, 98).

However, Ezekiel 37 alone and in its context is not intended to deliver a theology of general resurrection for all people. In the Old Testament, the concept of being resuscitated from the dead was believed to be something that only took place shortly after death (see 1 Kings 17:17-24; 2 Kings 4:18-37). Long-dead bones were a different matter entirely. This vision from Ezekiel 37 is not necessarily about a physical resurrection of the dead in the future but is a vision meant to instill hope for those living in the present. They have been saying to themselves, "Our bones are dried up, and our hope is lost; we are cut off completely" (v. 11). This vision is God's response to the people's hopelessness.

In the Western world, many churches feels as if they are now nothing but brittle bones, that their hope has been long misplaced, and that they are cut off from any possible future. In her book *Searching for Sunday*, Rachel Held Evans describes how she had cynically walked away from church yet felt God continually leading her back. At one point, she addresses the statistics many of us often hear about how the church in our culture is in precipitous decline:

> It has become popular in recent years for Christians to speak of the impending death of the church. . . . The alarm is not completely unfounded. Polls show the percentage of self-identified Christians in the United States has fallen from 86 percent to 76 percent

since 1990, while the percentage of people claiming no religious affiliation has doubled, rising to 16 percent. Young adults seem especially disinterested in faith, with nearly three out of every five young Christians disconnecting from church life after age fifteen.

I confess to citing these numbers ominously myself from time to time. . . . I may have uttered something along the lines of "adapt or die" in my writing once or twice. I may have jumped the gun and administered last rites.

But lately I've been wondering if a little death and resurrection might be just what the church needs right now, if maybe all this talk of waning numbers and shrinking influence means our empire-building days are over, and if maybe that's a good thing.

Death is something empires worry about, not something gardeners worry about. It's certainly not something resurrection people worry about. (Evans, 224–25)

The vision God gives Ezekiel is for resurrection people.

The Two Shall Become One (37:15-28)

After the vision of the dry bones coming to life through the power of God's *ruah* (spirit/breath/wind), Ezekiel is asked to perform his final act of street theater in the book. This demonstration is to address a lingering problem: while the people of God may be resurrected, there is still the issue of the divisions among them. However, "Yahweh is not the God of life, he is also the God of unity. If death can be reversed, so can division" (C. Wright 2001, 311–12). The theme of unity is what this passage is all about. Just as the Hebrew word *ruah* is the thread that runs throughout 37:1-14, the word for "one" (*ehad*) serves as the touchstone for this passage, referenced ten times in 37:15-28 (Duguid, 436).

Ezekiel is to pick up two pieces of wood (they may be ordinary sticks or ancient notepads). On one of them he is to write, "For Judah, and the Israelites associated with it" (v. 16a), and on the other he is to write, "For Joseph (the stick of Ephraim) and all the house of Israel associated with it" (v. 16b). Judah was the dominant tribe of the southern kingdom, and Ephraim was the dominant tribe of the northern kingdom (Block 1998, 402). With the two sticks in his hand, Ezekiel is to make them into one. This might be a miraculous event in which two sticks are transformed into one, or it could be a literal binding together of the two sticks.

The prophet is to hold up the stick in front of the people as they marvel about what it could mean. Ezekiel then preaches about the meaning of the stick and recalls many of the hopeful promises God has uttered throughout Ezekiel. These promises are a reversal of some of the issues that led to the divided kingdoms in the first place:

- The division was partly caused by a failure of leadership in which Rehoboam refused to serve the people with a servant's heart (1 Kings 12:7), but God will provide a Davidic king who will shepherd the people (Ezek 37:24).
- The kingdoms were divided because separate sanctuaries were erected (1 Kings 12:25-33), but God promises here in Ezekiel to establish a sanctuary that will theologically unify the people (v. 26) (Duguid, 436).

In the mind of God, there were never two kingdoms but always a unified people. This sign-act from Ezekiel serves to demonstrate that both the northern kingdom of Israel and the southern kingdom of Judah were never intended to be divided; both of them together are still God's chosen people.

In the movie *Lincoln* (dir. Steven Spielberg, Dreamworks Pictures, 2012), Abraham Lincoln reflects on the disunity of the United States in 1865. He speaks to two soldiers in the Union Army and begins to reference a law of mathematics from ancient Greece:

> Euclid's first common notion is this: "Things which are equal to the same thing are equal to each other." That's a rule of mathematical reasoning. It's true because it works; has done and always will do. In his book, Euclid says this is "self-evident." You see, there it is, even in that two-thousand-year-old book of mechanical law: it is a self-evident truth of things which are equal to the same thing, are equal to each other. We begin with equality. That's the origin, isn't it? That balance—that's fairness, that's justice.

Genuine Christian unity among divided people must begin with an acknowledgment of our equality in our standing before God. While we might allow secondary issues to divide us, our collective need for grace before God should unite us. As the saying goes, "The ground is level at the foot of the cross."

Many issues in our world today continue to divide us. As I write these words, we are a people deeply divided on issues such as racial justice, political identity, immigration, economic policy, abortion, and equality for people of all sexual orientations and gender expressions. Unity among the Body of Christ does not require that we agree on all of these issues, nor are we called to some superficial, sticky-sweet, fake unity that glosses over significant differences we may have. Instead, our calling is first to recognize that what unites us is our equal standing before God and then to move forward together to have difficult conversations in light of that equality. In his commentary on Ezekiel, Ian Duguid writes,

> True Christian unity does not flow from the top down, with high-level ecclesiastical committees and denominational leaders showing the way, nor does it flow from the bottom up, coming by means of grass-roots initiatives by individual church members. Rather, it flows from the center out: It comes from Christ-centered people discovering that they are, in fact, servants of a common Lord and King. (440)

What is required to heal the divisions in our world is a unity of purpose in serving Christ and a teachable spirit regarding those who differ from us. In her book *Dear White Peacemakers*, Black pastor and writer Osheta Moore calls for the Body of Christ to engage in conversations around racial justice that are necessary if we are to become the "Beloved Community" (as spoken about by Dr. Martin Luther King Jr.). She writes,

> Let us come together and be free. Let us come together and be nourished. Let us come together and offer unconditional positive regard because we have been unconditionally loved by God. Let us avoid the traps of either/or and violence. Let us become the Beloved Community, moving forward together with grit and grace. (102)

Conclusion

Both of the images we find in Ezekiel 37 are about restoration. They are about the healing of divisions. The valley of the dry bones symbolizes the divided souls of the people as they have been separated from any semblance of hope. But God dares to continue to speak words of good news even to lifeless bodies, bringing new life and resurrection. Ezekiel's demonstration with the two sticks initially illustrates the division that has existed among God's people. Yet the two kingdoms are made one and brought back into unity. This is not possible because of some superficial call for unity (which is usually just a call for conformity). This unity is only made possible through a shared and collective hope in the holiness of the Lord.

1. What kinds of "valleys" might we experience in our lives?

_____

_____

_____

_____

_____

2. Do you give much thought to the Holy Spirit in your life? What about in the life of your church?

_____

_____

_____

_____

_____

3. Why do you think pop culture is inundated with stories about zombies?

_____

_____

_____

_____

_____

4. *New Testament Connection:* Read 1 Corinthians 15:51-58. What connections do you see between the images of Ezekiel 37:1-14 and Paul's words about resurrection?

_____

_____

_____

_____

_____

5. How do you feel about Rachel Held Evans's ideas above? Where do you see hope in the church even in a season of decline?

_____

_____

_____

_____

_____

6. When you hear the word "unity," what images come to mind?

_____

_____

_____

_____

_____

7. Ezekiel wrote to a people who had been divided for hundreds of years, and he still believed unity was possible. What was the source of his hope?

_____

_____

_____

_____

_____

8. What are some secondary issues that easily divide God's people today?

_____

_____

_____

_____

_____

9. *New Testament Connection:* **Read John 17:20-24. How can we live out both Ezekiel's sign-act of the stick and the prayer of Jesus from the Gospel of John?**

_____

_____

_____

_____

_____

10. What part can you play in helping create the Beloved Community here on earth?

_____

_____

_____

_____

_____

The Lord Is There

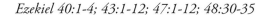

Ezekiel 40:1-4; 43:1-12; 47:1-12; 48:30-35

10

S e s s i o n

"The Word put on flesh and blood, and moved into the neighborhood."

—John 1:14, *The Message*

Sometimes when I am at a conference or training, there is a series of icebreaker questions designed to help us learn about one another. At a recent ministers' conference, one of the questions was, "What to you is the holiest place on earth?" One man described a mountaintop he had climbed once, and then a woman told about her favorite beach location. When it was my turn, I said, "It's a small, ranch-style house in Bollinger County, Missouri." It was the home of my grandpa and grandma Simmons. In addition to their modest home, Grandpa had built a wooden boardwalk that led to a gazebo with a porch swing, a concrete fire pit with the names of all of their grandchildren carved into the stone, and a field with mimosa trees where my cousins and I would gather. That property holds a thousand memories of childhood fun. But the holiest part were the two saintly grandparents who embodied grace, acceptance, and love. I still miss them. Because of my love for that place and those people, I can describe practically every nook and cranny at my grandparents' home.

When many readers come to Ezekiel 40–48, their eyes tend to glaze over a bit. It can be boring to read about building schematics, priestly duties, and the layout of a temple's kitchen. However, for the full force of this concluding section of Ezekiel to have any power, one has to imagine the deep love and affection that God's people had for the idea of a redeemed temple and city. We have already seen throughout the book that Ezekiel ministers to a people who feel as if they have lost their way of life, their religion, and their identity because of the brutality of exile. To prayerfully imagine and dream about a restored temple would have brought tears to their eyes. They would not gloss over these details but savor every measurement, soaking in the grandeur and beauty of this sacred space.

It's a fitting way for Ezekiel to end his book. Ezekiel began with chapters 1–24 laying out the argument for why the glory of God had vacated Jerusalem and the temple. The prophet then went on in chapters 25–32 to indict the surrounding nations. Next, he moved into oracles of hope in chapters 33–37 and to a final, eschatological defeat of evil (in the form of the mythical nations of Gog and Magog) in chapters 38–39. When we come to chapter 40, the stage has been set for a restored relationship between God and God's people. That is why the glory originally left: a broken relationship. This new temple and new city that Ezekiel describes is meant to be a metaphorical image for reconciliation between the people and their God. This is truly sacred space.

I do not have the space to expound on every detail or passage in Ezekiel 40–48. Instead, I will highlight four key passages that capture the heart of these nine chapters.

Ezekiel Finishes His Priestly Career (40:1-4)

We begin with another year of Ezekiel's precise dates for this vision: "In the twenty-fifth year of our exile, at the beginning of the year, on the tenth day of the month, in the fourteenth year after the city was struck down, on that very day, the hand of the LORD was upon me, and he brought me there" (40:1). Scholars have all kinds of theories about the significance of this specific date in Ezekiel. Some say that this specific date would have coincided with a Babylonian New Year celebration and that perhaps Ezekiel's vision is meant to counter the chest-thumping by the empire (Block 1998, 513). Others point out that the twenty-fifth year of the exile would have been the halfway point toward the Year of Jubilee (Lev 25:1-55), an Israelite celebration every fifty years that meant liberation and restitution, and perhaps the exiles assumed their freedom would come with the Jubilee. Perhaps casting this temple vision at the midpoint toward Jubilee would encourage the people that they were now on the downhill slope toward homecoming (Block 1998, 512).

For me, the most compelling aspect of this date formula in 40:1 involves the life of Ezekiel himself. If we jump all the way back to Ezekiel 1:1-3, we know that Ezekiel's inaugural vision took place when he was thirty years old. Raised in a priestly family, Ezekiel was expected to become a temple priest at the age of thirty. However, being separated from that sacred space in Jerusalem, his calling and vocation as he had always imagined them were not to be. Instead, as he sat by the River Chebar, God's glory came to him and called him to a new kind of ministry: a career of prophetic preaching that would require him to be innovative, creative, and entrepreneurial in ways he never could have imagined. Now, in the date formula from 40:1, we read that it has been twenty years since God ordained Ezekiel into this new ministry. In the Israelite religion, a temple priest would begin service at the age of thirty and would serve for twenty years. With this vision of a new temple, at age fifty, Ezekiel has fulfilled his calling (Odell, 486–87). He has fought the good fight. He has run the race. He has kept the faith.

All pastors and church leaders in the twenty-first century must recognize that we are a people in exile. The role of church has completely shifted in our world, and we must reimagine our notions of how to do ministry. As I write, we are still in the midst of the Covid-19 pandemic where churches have had to consider new ways to minister to people who are often separated from one another and their sacred spaces. However, just as Ezekiel the prophet said in his message, we are called to remind people that God is perhaps most present with God's people when they are scattered and when they feel forgotten. Our calling is to guard against the cynicism that so easily ensnares our world and to cling to the beating heart of flesh and hope that only God can provide.

This vision of a new temple takes place "upon a very high mountain" (40:2). Scripture is filled with examples of people encountering God on a mountain: Moses received the law on a mountain (Exod 19–34), Elijah spoke with God during his anxiety on a mountain (1 Kings 19), and Jesus began his ministry by delivering his sermon on a mount (Matt 5–7). Ezekiel receives this vision of a new temple on a metaphorical mountain that is the opposite of the theological territory of the "valley of the dry bones" in Ezekiel 37 (Duguid, 471–72). This prophet has endured the lowest of lows, but his book ends with a vision of hope in the highest of highs.

The Return of the King (43:1-12)

After hearing about many of the specifics of the new temple's schematics (40:5–42:20), Ezekiel looks to the east and sees a vision of God's glory, that fantastical, wheels-within-wheels, four-living-creatures image that he first encountered by the River Chebar (1:4-28) coming toward him. It comes from the east because the last time he saw this image, it had departed from the temple due to the people's idolatry and violence, and when it left it went east (10:19). The actions of the people toward God and toward their neighbors had both broken God's heart and defiled God's name (Fretheim, 68). But now the king has returned because the relationship is restored. The people have a new heart and a new spirit, and adherence to covenant loyalty is made possible by the grace of God.

When God returns to this new temple, God declares, "Mortal, this is the place of my throne and the place for the soles of my feet, where I will reside among the people of Israel forever" (43:7). In Isaiah's vision of God's holiness, he is taken to heaven and sees God seated on a throne (Isa 6), and in the Sermon on the Mount, Jesus speaks both of heaven as God's throne and also of the earth as God's footstool (Matt 5:34-35). Therefore, God's coming to the temple is the bringing together of heaven and earth. When God comes to this new and holy temple, heaven and earth meet and relationship with God is possible (Odell, 496–97). Christians believe that the cross of Jesus Christ accomplishes this marriage between heaven and earth in a new way so that his resurrection is the first-fruits of a new creation. In the New Testament letter of Ephesians, we are told that God's plan for the entire cosmos has always been about bringing together heaven and earth: "God has made known to us the mystery of his will, according to his good pleasure that he set forth in Christ, as a plan for the fullness of time, to gather up all things in him, things in heaven and things on earth" (Eph 1:9-10).

When God returns to the temple to sit on the throne and to rest God's feet, Ezekiel is then told to preach to the people about all that he has seen. And the response is surprising: "let them be ashamed of their iniquities" (43:10). In this midst of this mighty vision of a hopeful future, why are we returning yet again to the topic of shame? Shame is a theme in the book of Ezekiel and is often a response by the people even to the restorative actions of God (see 16:61-63 and 36:31-32). Margaret Odell effectively argues that the shame of the people here in 43:1-12 has a necessary and even redemptive purpose. In the face of the holiness and set-apartness of God, only conviction of the people's sins of idolatry and violence can serve as the first step in reconciliation with God. She says, "only when the house of Israel feels shame for what it has done will it be able to hear Ezekiel's account of the temple and respond accordingly" (Odell,

499). However, because this is a fantastical vision of an ideal future, the shame felt by the people has a penultimate quality: "Yahweh does insist that Israel bear its shame for all that it has done; but even this burdensome self-loathing will become a thing of the past" (Odell, 499–500). That is the power of the gospel in our lives. Yes, it begins with a feeling of conviction of our own brokenness, but the true gospel does not leave us to wallow in our total depravity. Instead, grace lifts us out of that mire and places before us a heavenly dream: "God will wipe away every tear from their eyes. Death will be no more; mourning and crying and pain will be no more, for the first things have passed away" (Rev 21:4).

The River of Life (47:1-12)

Ezekiel 43:13–46:24 lays out various kinds of regulations and laws that will pertain to the vision of the new temple, including a new altar, the governance of a new priestly order, and the regulation of holy days in this new liturgical space. When we come to Ezekiel 47:1-12, we encounter another prophetic vision meant to instruct us about the nature and character of God.

The prophet Ezekiel is brought back to the entrance of the temple and hears an unfamiliar noise. It's the sound of trickling water flowing from the threshold. It's not an impressive amount of water. The flow of the liquid is described with the Hebrew word *mepakkim*, which is an onomatopoeia that literally means "to be poured from a bottle" (Darr, 412). However, Ezekiel begins to follow this thin line of water. Soon, the water widens and deepens to cover his ankles. A little farther it is up to his knees, then up to his waist, and finally it becomes a surging river that cannot be crossed. The idea of water flowing from a temple was not an unprecedented image in Ezekiel's day. Many temples in the ancient Near East were constructed on springs to symbolize the deities' connection to the primordial waters of creation myths (Walton and Keener, 1415–16).

Ezekiel's image of a river flowing from the temple of God also has connections to the Israelite stories of creation. The book of Genesis speaks of rivers flowing through the garden of Eden (Gen 2:10-14), and Ezekiel's river has creative and generative qualities. The river flows into the Arabah (the basin featuring the Dead Sea). This holy river brings healing that transforms the briny Dead Sea into a lush, paradisaical oasis. The Dead Sea teems with sea life of all kinds, but the resurrection of this body of water also brings with it the return of economic possibility since the natural resource provides what is necessary for the return of a workforce of fishing and even salt-mining. In his diatribes against Tyre, Ezekiel ranted about the unjust and exploitative economic practices that had come to dominate Tyre's economy (26:1-5). In Ezekiel's vision of a new temple, the restoration of the relationship between God and God's people has an impact on both the ecology and the economy. Creation is restored to its intended flourishing role, and the economy of the new vision provides job security for the community (Davis, 126).

The book of Revelation reflects Ezekiel's vision in the ideas of the new heaven and new earth. As in Ezekiel's vision, John sees a river flowing from God's presence that brings life to creation. Both Ezekiel and Revelation's rivers also serve as symbols for the love of God that is accessible to more than just one group of people: it is "for the healing of the nations" (Rev 22:2). These images always push back and flow against any efforts made to limit the grace of God.

For Christians, the image of this holy river also belongs with other biblical images that remind us of the baptismal waters. Alongside the aforementioned rivers flowing through the garden of Eden (Gen 2:10-14), the eschatological river of John's Apocalypse (Rev 22:1-5), and the prophet Zechariah's message of "living waters" flowing from Jerusalem (Zech 14:8-9), Ezekiel 47:1-12 serves as a reminder that Christian faith takes ordinary water and sees within it the very presence of God's healing grace and love. As Ronald Byars writes,

> The church's experience of the sacrament of baptism brings together these several streams derived from eschatological images in both testaments and joins them in a rite that wraps them all together in a way that is fundamentally doxological, in praise for God's work in the past, the present, and the age to come. (111)

Like all powerful biblical images, Ezekiel's image of this river of life does not simply sit on a shelf in the past, nor is it cast so far into the future as to be irrelevant. It transforms us and invites us into a different way of being human in the present, seeing the world as already covered in the waters of God's grace.

Yahweh Shamma (48:30-35)

Ezekiel's vision of the new temple ends with a listing of the gates of the city allotted to the tribes of Israel. The final note of the vision (and of the book itself) is when we learn that this is not just a new temple but a redeemed and transformed city that is given a new name: *Yahweh Shamma* ("The LORD Is There," v. 35). Throughout the visions of Ezekiel 40–48, it is clear that this new city and new temple are places of both restoration and safety. For Ezekiel and the exiles who are processing the trauma of exile, this would have been true gospel for their souls. The first act of care a trauma victim must receive is a tangible place of safety and an assurance that their trauma can no longer reoccur. This vision of Ezekiel and the assurance of God's permanent presence in the city provides the promise that no longer shall God's people be victimized by power-hungry empires.

For Ezekiel and the exiles to whom he has ministered, what better news could they hear? These are people who have felt marginalized and forgotten. Ezekiel has laid before them an image of a new temple that brings healing to the broken relationships between the people, creation, and their God. Ezekiel, who has seen God's glory depart from the temple, now finds a permanent home in this new temple alongside the people God loves so dearly.

Conclusion

Each Advent season, our churches rightly focus on Immanuel ("God with us") as we remember that in Jesus Christ, we find the "image of the invisible God" (Col 1:15). That is still good news for us. When we are overwhelmed by the brokenness of our world, "The Lord Is There." When the relentless march of time finds us and we say goodbye to those we love, "The Lord Is There." When we are victims of unjust or marginalizing policies in our world, "The Lord Is There." That is the good news: the Creator of the universe does not leave us in our brokenness but finds us there. That is the incarnational hope of the gospel, and it is the message of hope that Ezekiel speaks even in the midst of the brokenness of exile. In the words of *The Message*, "The Word put on flesh and blood and moved into the neighborhood" (John 1:14).

1. What is a sacred space in your life?

_____
_____
_____
_____
_____

2. What are some areas of our lives in which we tend to focus on the smallest details?

_____
_____
_____
_____
_____

3. How do you think Ezekiel has served as a priest and prophet to the exiles?

_____
_____
_____
_____
_____

4. *New Testament Connection:* Read 1 Peter 2:9. What is God's vision for the priesthood?

_____
_____
_____
_____
_____

5. What role does conviction play in Christian formation?

_____
_____
_____
_____
_____

6. *New Testament Connection:* Read Ephesians 1:9-10. When we recognize that God's ultimate purpose is to bring together heaven and earth, how should it change the way we live?

_____

_____

_____

_____

_____

7. What role should Christians play in advocating for the health of our bodies of water and access to water for all people?

_____

_____

_____

_____

_____

8. *New Testament Connection:* Read Revelation 22:1-5. How do you think John was influenced by Ezekiel's vision?

_____

_____

_____

_____

_____

9. When have you needed to know "The Lord Is There"?

_____

_____

_____

_____

_____

10. How would you summarize the ministry of Ezekiel?

_____

_____

_____

_____

_____

Works Cited

APA. "Narrative Exposure Therapy (NET)." *Clinical Practice Guideline for the Treatment of Posttraumatic Stress Disorder.* apa. org/ptsd-guideline/treatments/narrative-exposure-therapy.

Berry, Wendell. *The Gift of Good Land: Further Essays Cultural and Agricultural.* San Francisco: North Point Press, 1981.

———. "How to Be a Poet." *Poetry Foundation.* poetryfoundation. org/poetrymagazine/poems/41087/how-to-be-a-poet.

Blenkinsopp, Joseph. *Ezekiel.* Interpretation: A Bible Commentary for Teaching and Preaching. Louisville: Westminster John Knox, 1990.

Block, Daniel I. *The Book of Ezekiel, Chapters 1–24.* The New International Commentary on the Old Testament. Grand Rapids: Eerdmans, 1997.

———. *The Book of Ezekiel, Chapters 25–48.* The New International Commentary on the Old Testament. Grand Rapids: Eerdmans, 1998.

Bolsinger, Tod. *Canoeing the Mountains: Christian Leadership in Uncharted Territory.* Westmont, IL: IVP Books, 2018.

Bonhoeffer, Dietrich. *The Cost of Discipleship.* (London: SCM Press, 1959).

Bowen, Nancy R. *Ezekiel.* Abingdon Old Testament Commentaries. Nashville: Abingdon, 2010.

Brueggemann, Walter. *Cadences of Home: Preaching Among Exiles.* Louisville: Westminster John Knox, 1997.

————. *Hopeful Imagination: Prophetic Voices in Exile*. Minneapolis: Fortress, 1986.

————. *Living Toward a Vision: Biblical Reflections on* Shalom. Cleveland: Pilgrim Press, 1982.

————. *Money and Possessions*. Interpretation: Resources for the Use of Scripture in the Church. Louisville: Westminster John Knox, 2016.

————. "Reflections on Ezekiel," *Christian Century*. 30 November 1998. 96–98.

Byars, Ronald P. *The Sacraments in Biblical Perspective*. Interpretation: Resources for the Use of Scripture in the Church. Louisville: Westminster John Knox, 2011.

Christianity Today. *The Rise and Fall of Mars Hill*. Podcast. christianitytoday.com/ct/podcasts/rise-and-fall-of-mars-hill/.

"ConAgra Foods' Feeding Children Better Foundation." *Encyclopedia.com*. encyclopedia.com/marketing/encyclopedias-almanacs-transcripts-and-maps/conagra-foods-feeding-children-better-foundation.

Creach, Jerome F. D. *Violence in Scripture*. Interpretation: Resources for the Use of Scripture in the Church. Louisville: Westminster John Knox, 2013.

Darr, Kathyrn Pfisterer. "The Book of Ezekiel: Introduction, Commentary, and Reflections." In *The New Interpreter's Bible*, vol. 6. Nashville: Abingdon, 2001.

Davis, Ellen F. *Biblical Prophecy: Perspectives on Christian Theology, Discipleship, and Ministry*. Interpretation: Resources for the Use of Scripture in the Church. Louisville: Westminster John Knox, 2014.

De La Torre, Miguel A., and Albert Hernandez. *The Quest for the Historical Satan*. Minneapolis: Fortress, 2011.

Dorfman, Ariel. *Feeding on Dreams: Confessions of an Unrepentant Exile*. Boston: Houghton Mifflin Harcourt, 2011.

Duguid, Ian. *Ezekiel*. The NIV Application Commentary. Grand Rapids: Zondervan, 1999.

Evans, Rachel Held. *Searching for Sunday: Loving, Leaving, and Finding the Church*. Nashville: Thomas Nelson, 2015.

Francis of Assisi. "All Creatures of Our God and King." 1225. In *Celebrating Grace: Hymnal for Baptist Worship*, 2010. # 307.

Fretheim, Terence E. *The Suffering of God: An Old Testament Perspective*. Overtures to Biblical Theology. Minneapolis: Fortress, 1984.

Gilot, Frances, and Carlton Lake. *Life with Picasso*. New York: New American Library, 1965.

Harris, Colin. "Injustice and Idolatry—Twin Sins?" *Good Faith Media*. September 15, 2020. goodfaithmedia.org/injustice-and-idolatry-twin-sins/.

Hicks, Edward. *The Peaceable Kingdom*. Pennsylvania Academy of the Fine Arts. pafa.org/museum/collection/item/peaceable-kingdom.

Jenson, Robert W. *Ezekiel*. Brazos Theological Commentary on the Bible. Ada, MI: Brazos Press, 2009.

Knight, Paul. "Letter: Quote from Humphrey, not Gandhi." November 11, 2016. *Columbian*. columbian.com/news/2016/nov/11/letter-quote-from-humphrey-not-gandhi/.

Lewis, C. S. *The Lion, the Witch, and the Wardrobe*. London: Geoffrey Bles, 1950.

Odell, Margaret S. *Ezekiel*. Smyth & Helwys Bible Commentary. Macon: Smyth & Helwys, 2005.

Orwell, George. *The Collected Essays, Journalism and Letters of George Orwell*. Edited by Sonia Orwell and Ian Angus. 4 vols. New York: Harcourt Brace Jovanovich, 1968.

Middleton, J. Richard. *A New Heaven and a New Earth: Reclaiming Biblical Eschatology*. Ada, MI: Baker Academic, 2014.

Moore, Osheta. *Dear White Peacemakers: Dismantling Racism with Grit and Grace*. Independence, MO: Herald Press, 2021.

Scazzero, Peter. *Emotionally Healthy Spirituality: It's Impossible to be Spiritually Mature while Remaining Emotionally Immature*. Grand Rapids: Zondervan, 2006.

Sinek, Simon. *Leaders Eat Last: Why Some Teams Pull Together and Others Don't*. New York: Portfolio, 2014.

Smith-Christopher, Daniel L. *A Biblical Theology of Exile*. Overtures to Biblical Theology. Minneapolis: Fortress, 2002.

Thurman, Howard. *Disciplines of the Spirit*. New York: Harper & Row, 1963.

Vatican. "Homily of Pope Francis." November 1, 2014. The Holy See. vatican.va/content/francesco/en/homilies/2014/documents/papa-francesco_20141101_omelia-ognissanti.html.

Wall, Cara. *The Dearly Beloved: A Novel*. New York: Simon and Schuster, 2019.

Walton, John H., and Craig S. Keener, eds. *The NRSV Cultural Backgrounds Study Bible*. Grand Rapids: Zondervan, 2019.

Ward, Jesmyn. *Sing, Unburied, Sing: A Novel*. New York: Scribner, 2017.

Weems, Renita J. *Battered Love: Marriage, Sex, and Violence in the Hebrew Prophets*. Overtures to Biblical Theology. Minneapolis: Fortress, 1995.

West, Cornel. "Askwith Forum: Cornel West—Spiritual Blackout, Imperial Meltdown, Prophetic Fightback." Address at Harvard Graduate School of Education. Askwith Forum Lecture Series, October 4, 2017. youtube.com/watch?v=zuxqhsrCGeg.

Wright, Christopher J. H. *"Here Are Your Gods": Faithful Discipleship in Idolatrous Times*. Westmone, IL: IVP Academic, 2020.

———. *The Message of Ezekiel: A New Heart and a New Spirit*. The Bible Speaks Today. Westmont, IL: IVP Academic, 2001.

———. *Old Testament Ethics for the People of God*. Westmont, IL: IVP Academic, 2004.

Wright, N. T. *Surprised by Hope: Rethinking Heaven, the Resurrection, and the Mission of the Church*. San Francisco: HarperOne, 2008.

———. *After You Believe: Why Christian Character Matters*. San Francisco: HarperOne, 2010.